THE BAFFLED PARENT'S GUIDE TO
COACHING YOUTH
FOOTBALL

Look for these other Baffled Parent's Guides

THE BAFFLED PARENT'S
GUIDE TO
COACHING YOUTH
FOOTBALL

Paul Pasqualoni
Head Coach, Syracuse University
with Jim McLaughlin

Ragged Mountain Press/McGraw-Hill

Camden, Maine • New York • Chicago • San Francisco
Lisbon • London • Madrid • Mexico City • Milan • New Delhi
San Juan • Seoul • Singapore • Sydney • Toronto

To Jim and Virginia McLaughlin—the coaches of my life.
JIM McLAUGHLIN

The McGraw·Hill Companies

DOC 10 9 8 7 6 5 4 3 2 1

Copyright © 2002 Nomad Communications

Library of Congress Cataloging-in-Publication Data
Pasqualoni, Paul.
  The baffled parent's guide to coaching youth football / Paul
Pasqualoni with Jim McLaughlin.
       p.   cm. — (The baffled parent's guides)
Includes bibliographical references (p.   ) and index.
  ISBN 0-07-137219-9
  1. Youth league football—Coaching. I. McLaughlin, Jim, 1946– II.
Title. III. Series.
  GV959.6 .P37 2002
  796.332´07´7—dc21   2002008624

Questions regarding the content of this book should be addressed to
Ragged Mountain Press
P.O. Box 220
Camden, ME 04843
www.raggedmountainpress.com

Questions regarding the ordering of this book should be addressed to
The McGraw-Hill Companies
Customer Service Department
P.O. Box 547
Blacklick, OH 43004
Retail customers: 1-800-262-4729
Bookstores: 1-800-722-4726
Photographs by Michael J. Okoniewski except pages 26 (2), 46 (2), 47 (2), 50, 62 (2), 63 (2),
    64, 68 (2), 69 (left and middle), 114 by Monty Rand
Illustrations by Accurate Art

Contents

Part Two

Drills: The Foundation for Growth, Happiness, and a Coach's Peace of Mind

A player fully equipped and ready for action.

Introduction

So, you're a Baffled Parent. When your son begged you to let him play football, you drove him to the league sign-up and waited to hear all about the upcoming season. Instead, you discovered that his team didn't have a coach, and in a moment of weakness you agreed to step in. Suddenly you're the newest coach in the league, even though you've never actually *played* football, and you've definitely never coached before. Panic sets in. All those terms, all those positions to understand: left guard, split end, wide-out, nickel back, quarterback, halfback, fullback, I-back, H-back. All those teams to organize: offensive team, defensive team, punt teams, kick-return team, hands team. And all those formations: pro, slot, wing, T, split back, one-back, no-back. Worried?

Don't be. You're about to be infected by the disease of coaching the "Great North American Game," and there's no cure. In this game the skills are so diverse and varied that just about every youngster can find a niche and contribute to a successful effort. In football the most important elements are desire, effort, and discipline, and the rewards are limited only by the length of the practice, the games, and the season. You'll need to supply enthusiasm as the necessary catalyst for commitment.

Welcome to coaching. What you're doing right now is what all of us do: learn from others. Whether you're new to coaching or not, looking for new ideas and techniques is an ongoing goal for all who guide youngsters in their pursuit of a successful experience in our game. If you think you need help, don't worry. Help is at hand. This book is designed to help any coach have a successful season—and by successful we don't mean more wins than losses. The advice, games, and drills here are aimed at helping you teach children the basics of football, sportsmanship, teamwork, discipline, safety, and, above all else, the fun and rewards of the game.

The advice and drills in this book are designed for coaching 6- to 12-year-old players. This age group includes kids who've played only touch football on the playground right through to players who've played league football for six years. These players represent a lot of fun and a great deal of challenge. Some will know more about the game than you, while others will need help strapping on their pads. Some kids will be making impressive tackles and airborne catches while others will be afraid of contact and will run from the ball. Some will be enthusiastic while others will prefer the bench. All of your players, however, want to enjoy their time on the team. They can experience individual development, share in the thrill of contributing to team victory, and learn how adversity contributes to resolve. These are the challenges we deal with throughout this book.

Coaching Youth Football: The Baffled Parent's Guide is like an organized assistant, providing advice on everything from the philosophy of the game to the logistical hurdles necessary to get the season going. It also contains a system of skill development, from the basics to more advanced skills, complete with a grab bag of drills and clear illustrations to guide you. Though the book takes you through the season in a logical way, you can also use it in segments as specific needs or issues arise.

Part One: Coaching 101: The Coach's Start-Up Kit will introduce you to the game and take you through the beginning of the season. You may need advice on how to establish yourself as the coach in a positive and encouraging manner and how to create an environment that teaches respect. Everything you need to know is in chapter 1, Creating an Atmosphere of Good Habits. Need to brush up on the game of football? We provide a crash course on the game in chapter 2. Chapter 3 gives you information on setting up the team. Chapters 4 through 6, emphasizing essential skills, provide the foundation for what you need to know about skills and drills. In chapter 4 we discuss defensive systems, examine the alignments and structures needed to defend against any offense, and provide an introduction to skills and instructional drills. In chapter 5 we explain offensive formations, along with philosophies of the running and passing games and a precise explanation of the techniques your players need to learn and the drills to master them. In chapter 6 we focus on the kicking game, including the formations, philosophies, and drills for any young player.

Chapter 7 offers tips and ideas for running football practices. In chapter 8, Tips for Game Day, we'll assist you in organizing your team from the pregame huddle to the final whistle. And finally, if you need help dealing with the many parent, player, and coaching issues that may arise within the season, we're there for you in chapter 9, Dealing with Parents.

In Part Two: Drills: The Foundation for Growth, Happiness, and a Coach's Peace of Mind, you'll find specific step-by-step drills to help with fundamentals and with defensive and offensive skills. This is what football coaches dream about. These are all techniques and drills used by amateur and professional coaches each fall throughout the world of tackle football. Use them, modify them, and fit them into your situation, because each team is different, and each coach has a particular personality.

Broadly speaking, the drills and plays contained within this book are appropriate for youth football players between the ages of 6 and 12. Intensity levels and variations of them will alter their complexity and skill level.

Throughout the book you'll find helpful Question and Answer sections that address common and hard-to-handle issues and sidebars designed to encourage you and provide additional information. Finally, you'll find referee signals, a glossary of football terms, a list of resources available to you, and a detailed index helpful in locating advice on specific problems.

Be aware: this book is an assistant; you are the coach. For the book to be helpful, you must mold it to your personality and coaching style. One coach might be pure enthusiasm, and another might be calm and quiet. But either can be a good coach just as either can be a bad one. This book is also a tool. If you use it effectively, it will make your work easier and a lot more fun.

Always remind yourself that your goal is to provide a fun and rewarding experience for you and your team. Continue to stress good habits and never stop encouraging your players. Emphasize strong effort, and always stress and emulate courtesy and respect for one another, your opponents, and the refs. As the coach, you're also your players' teacher. By what you say and especially by what you do, you can teach them the importance of teamwork and the development of safe football skills. You have the opportunity to teach the value of competition, that winning and losing are both part of the positive experience, and that having fun is the name of the game.

With or without coaching credentials you have the responsibility and capability of teaching your players lessons about football and lessons about life. You and they have the opportunity to make great progress and to enjoy a successful season.

To set off on the right foot, here are five keys to being a good coach:

Remember the Scouting motto: always be prepared. Every time you walk out onto the field, have a plan for what you want to accomplish during practice that day. Know what drills and plays you'll work on and how long you want to spend on each one. Make sure that you're familiar enough with what you plan to do so that you can present it clearly. By organizing your thoughts and preparing a practice plan ahead of time, you'll keep the kids moving, interested, and learning.

On the other hand, be flexible: if it isn't working, do something else. You don't have to be a psychiatrist to judge when kids are motivated and having fun, and when they are bored. You can have a great practice plan on paper, but if for some reason it's not going well, be ready to change your plan and move on to something else.

Good words go a long way: keep it positive. Everyone loves praise and encouragement. Make sure that one of your cardinal rules is that the coach is the only person *ever* to criticize a player—and then only in a positive, constructive way. Kids should never criticize other kids. And remember that kids never can hear enough of "Great job," "Nice try," "Good work." Positive encouragement is vital to a positive experience.

Keep your energy level high. You need to match the energy level of the kids you'll be coaching. No matter what might be happening in other parts of your life, psych yourself up before each practice so that you're fully engaged in the practice or game from the moment you step onto the field. Your players will feed off your energy, and everyone will have a better practice or game because of it.

Keep your eyes open and get to know your team. One of the best ways to learn to coach your team effectively is to observe. Watch your players carefully; get to know their personalities. You'll learn a lot just by watching how they react and interact with each other. And be sure to learn every player's name right away—they need the recognition and respond positively to it.

PART ONE

Coaching 101:
The Coach's Start-Up Kit

CHAPTER 1

Creating an Atmosphere of Good Habits

Before we talk about what habits are useful and demonstrate how to create an atmosphere that promotes them while discouraging bad habits, it's important that we take a look at the concept of "team." What is a team? What are the responsibilities of membership on a team? In other words, what does it mean to be a teammate? Most importantly for you, how do you take thirty youngsters with at least six different skill levels and make them into one team?

A team is a group of individuals who have joined together to pursue a common goal or interest. In pursuing this end, the members agree to a mutually accepted set of "givens" and "assumptions" that they will follow to promote the goals of the group. The givens and assumptions are a set of prerequisites, starting with a commitment to prompt attendance at all practices. Teams are often compared to machines: parts working together to create a final product. The better the machine's parts, the more efficiently it performs. The longer the machine runs, the more "oiled" it becomes. A good team is a well-oiled machine, where each player develops an appreciation for the commitment of others and a responsibility to uphold his end of the effort. This is the key to creating team chemistry, which in turn is the key to a successful football program.

In order to accomplish this, the players must adopt a disciplined approach to learning and performance. They work hard, practice hard, and play hard because they want to be trusted members of the team, someone their teammates can count on. Players take their rewards from the performance of the group and develop a pride in their contributions.

Along with the development of team chemistry is a sense of altruism. Bo Schembechler, the much-respected former head coach at the University of Michigan, used to say that only three things really counted: The Team, The Team, and The Team. We can think of many sports that are much more fun to practice than football. Getting into all that equipment on hot days, or when snow is flying, or in rain and mud takes a special level of understanding by each player that his teammates are counting on him even though he might want to do other things. When the coach says he needs an offensive tackle, the player who dreamed of throwing touchdown passes learns that team success may necessitate putting personal wants aside for the betterment of the group.

There are only two forces that work on an athletic team: those that bring players together and those that pull them apart. No matter what happens, from the biggest event to the smallest incident, these forces are the decisive factors. More than skills or talents of the individuals on your team, what determines their success is the ratio of these two forces. We can all relate stories of talented groups that fell far short of their goals due to the lack of a good team dynamic and, conversely, teams of lesser individual abilities that reached great heights because they became a team.

Coaching Football

This season may be your players' first experience with organized football. No coach is burdened with a more singular and stereotypical image of the whistle-blowing tyrant than a football coach. But the hard-nosed, hard-talking drill instructor at this level of play is more often than not someone masking a lack of understanding of youngsters and the game with bravado and intimidation. Don't be misled—football is a contact sport, and you'll be asking novice players to perform some techniques demanding displays of courage that, at the very least, may be out of character. But fear of failure plus fear of the coach do not add up to successful players. The key to working with most kids is to be yourself, be full of enthusiasm, and judge effort on an individual basis. Remember you're teaching your players, and good teaching techniques are no less important here than in any other form of education. The kids will do anything you ask them to do—it's your job to ask them to do the things they can do and to teach them how to do what they don't already know.

Starting the Season

"Welcome to the team, fellas. This is what I expect from you, and this is what you can count on from me."

At the start of the season, have a get-together with your prospective players and their parents. Whatever rules and regulations you want for your team need to be presented at this time. This will alert everyone to what your expectations are for team members. It's a good way to give relevance to your policies and to alert team members and their parents as to the consequence of noncompliance. Schedules, practice times, and the players' and coaches' phone numbers can be distributed. It may be a good idea to talk to other coaches in your league about their expectations for comparison. It's important to make your rules fair and enforceable and related to your team. Remember you're coaching a football team, and the habits you're forging should be directly related to team matters. Consistent application of team rules is one of the cornerstones of being an effective leader. It's far better not to have a rule than to have one you don't enforce.

Coaching Habits

We believe the definition of effective leadership has to include the ability as a coach to demonstrate a caring style with your team as a whole and your players as individuals. However, it's also critical that you instill in your team a work ethic, or what's called *team pride*. Team pride is the idea that satisfaction in one's effort will promote the best in practice and playing habits on a consistent basis. Good habits must be coached, constantly reinforced, and repeatedly acknowledged in the most positive terms until they become ingrained in youngsters as part of their athletic personality. For your part, the team needs to believe that the personnel decisions you are making are made with the best interest of the team foremost in your mind.

You cannot overemphasize the importance of practice time. All football games are won on the practice field. This axiom is universally accepted by all coaches. The process of preparation is one of the most valuable lessons that football coaches can instill in their athletes. The adage "failure to prepare is preparing to fail" is particularly important in football. *Never call off practice.* This is probably an extreme statement, but practice should only be canceled in the most extreme, uncontrollable situations. Have alternatives for weather problems or facility problems. For example, tell your players, "If the field lights are out, we'll have a blackboard session in my garage." Remember that early planning can overcome many obstacles. The point is that if practices are canceled, their importance will be diminished in the eyes of your players, and you'll soon be dealing with player excuses for missing practice.

Keep your practice time within a window that will maximize teaching retention. Practices can reach a point of diminishing returns. Practices that go beyond two hours are approaching this point. Physical fatigue and mental saturation lead to a level of disinterest that has a negative effect on good habit development and the retention of skills and assignments, and it may increase the risk of injury, especially with younger athletes. (For more on practices, see chapter 7.)

The Coach

This book began with the premise that your child lured you to football registration, and that *you* agreed to coach. One of the facts of life you're about to notice is that your child is now under different pressures, as the coach's

Safety

There are a number of youth football injuries every year. According to the Centers for Disease Control and Prevention (CDC), many of them can be prevented if safety gear is used properly and players follow the rules of the game.

Here are some safety tips the CDC recommends.

- Suggest to parents that they take their child to get a physical exam prior to the start of preseason camp; their doctor can assess any potential injury risks.

- Make sure players wear all required safety gear for games and practices.

- Be sure that all players warm up and stretch adequately before practice begins.

- Teach your players *not* to play through pain. In case of injury, follow the doctor's orders for the child's recovery and make sure the child gets his or her doctor's OK before returning to practices and games.

- First aid should be available at all practices and games.

- You, as the coach, should enforce all rules of the game; watch for illegal play and encourage safety.

- And, as we stress throughout this book, keep football fun: too much emphasis on winning can make young players push too hard and risk injury.

Local youth football organizations may establish rules to meet their specific situations and needs, such as the numbering of linemen's shirts, whether coaches are allowed on the field, playing time, practice restrictions, and play restrictions. These rules must never lessen established safety procedures and regulations.

son or daughter, than the rest of the team. Most of this became unavoidable the second you accepted the coaching post. It's important for team morale and cohesion that you treat all the players the same. One way to help create a more professional atmosphere is have every player call you "Coach," including your child. It's a title you'll share with some of the most successful people in our country, people who have dedicated their lives to working with young people in all forms of athletic pursuits. Be proud to wear this title and have a great time with your team, Coach!

A Perfect Fit

If there's one aspect of coaching this sport with which you absolutely need to get expert help, it is the fitting of protective equipment, especially the helmet and shoulder pads. At this age, football players have many safety advantages: they're relatively close to the ground, they're too small to generate much torque, and they're the most padded of all age-group athletes. The biggest concern is protection of the head and neck. Helmets have come a long way in their ability to protect players, but they need to be fitted by an expert. Look at the manufacturer's label in the helmet you are using and call the manufacturer's representatives. They can instruct you on where to go for the best possible fit of their product or how to do the fitting yourself. They'll be more than happy to assist you. Don't let anyone who cannot produce valid credentials fit your players.

Questions and Answers

Q. What sort of legal liability am I assuming by taking on this role as coach?

A. Most leagues have insurance that will cover your players in case of injury. As part of this coverage, you, as the coach, are covered for liabilities that can accompany coaching a sport. It is certainly in your best interest to verify exactly what's covered in this policy and when you're protected. Make sure that you also inquire about coverage for players that you or other coaches transport in private cars to and from games or practices.

Q. There's a player who comes to practice late on a regular basis. He is not very good, so I have not made much of his tardiness. Am I making a mistake in not dealing with this situation?

A. Even though this player may not be a "star," he is still a part of the organization and needs to abide by team rules and regulations. By disciplining him, you may give him a sense of worth that he may not be feeling because he sees himself as a noncontributor. Impressing upon him that he is a valuable part of the team by holding him accountable may be the motivation he needs to get to practice. Letting things slide in regard to team rules will always come back to haunt you. Be consistent and give out penalties according to circumstance, but always apply the rules.

Q. I have a parent who is critical of my coaching. How do I deal with criticism?

A. If you're comfortable with what you're doing, are organized, and have a sound plan, continue to work hard and enjoy your team. There are always critics. Remember, you're working for the kids on your team and no one else. Trying to please anyone else is not part of your job description.

Q. How should I handle the athletic supporter debate? Some parents insist their child wear one; others don't.

A. Opinions vary on this subject, so it's best to leave it up to the parents' discretion.

Before Hitting the Field: Football in a Nutshell

The Basics: The Struggle for Land

Let's now turn to the rules of football. Unlike many other sports, tackle football can be played properly only in the most organized of settings. Youth, Pop Warner (a national league), middle and high school, college, and professional leagues are the venues for our game. Most players, except the most talented, will end their playing days with high school graduation. It's truly a fleeting experience, yet it's the nation's most popular school sport, with nearly a million participants each fall in high schools alone.

One can envision a long-ago soccer match where some frustrated player broke the rules, picked up the ball, and ran toward the goal. Another player on the opposite team retaliated and brought the renegade runner to the ground. Both teams decided that this looked like a lot of fun, and rugby was born. American football, the game that began in 1869 with Princeton playing Rutgers, has its origins in rugby. It has evolved into the highly organized, complex game we have come to know today. Although the game is played with many variations, this book concentrates on eleven-player tackle football.

Simply put, the sport is a game of struggle for the acquisition of territory. The playing surface dimensions are adjusted for the age and size of the players involved, but the layout of a football field is generally the same. For the purposes of this introduction, we'll use the high school field as the pattern. The game is played on a rectangle 360 feet long by 160 feet wide. Feet, however, are rarely used in the language of the *gridiron* (another name for the football field), where yards are the official unit of measure for the game. Each *end zone* is 10 yards in length, and the field of play is 100 yards long from *goal line* to goal line. Between the goal lines, the field is marked with lines from sideline to sideline every 5 yards. On each of these lines, exactly one-third of the way in from the sideline (53 feet, 4 inches), a line called the *inbounds marker* (or *hash mark*) is drawn across the yard lines. If

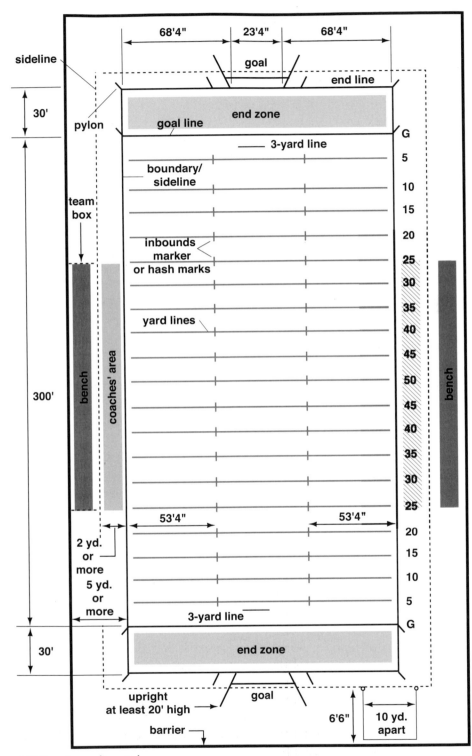

Field dimensions and terminology.

a down ends between this line and the sideline, the ball is moved to the inbounds marker for the next play.

The Object of the Game

The object of the game of football is to score points by taking the ball into your opponent's end zone (a *touchdown*) or by kicking it over the crossbar of the goal posts located on the end line of your opponent's end zone (a *field goal*). The team with the most points at the end of the game wins.

Downs

The down is the basic unit of the game. The *down*, or play, begins when the offensive team moves the ball forward and ends with a score, a tackle, an incomplete pass, or when the person in possession of the ball goes out-of-bounds. Once a team gains possession of the ball, it has four downs to either get the ball across the opponent's goal line or acquire at least 10 yards of territory. If the team gains the 10 yards or more within its allotted four downs, it gets a *first down*, which gives the team four more downs in which to move the ball.

During a down, a team may choose to run with the ball, to pass the ball from one player to another, or to kick the ball. Kicking the ball, however, causes the team to lose possession and is usually a concession that making the first down is not probable. Kicking the ball away is usually

A Typical Series of Downs

A set of downs may go something like this:

Your team's offense is on its own 35-yard line, meaning it has 65 yards to go in order to reach the defense's end zone for a touchdown.

It's *first and 10*. A pass attempt is made and completed by the offense. There's a gain of 4 yards. Your team is now at the 39-yard line.

It's now *second and 6* (meaning you need to gain 6 yards to get the next first down). You try a running play, but the defense stops the offense behind the *line of scrimmage* for a loss of a yard! (Yes, not only can an offense gain yards, but it can lose yardage, too.) The offense is now back at the 38-yard line.

Now it is *third and 7*. The offense needs 7 yards to get the first down. If you don't move the ball at least this far, it will be fourth down, and because your team is still perilously close to your own end zone, your offense will likely have to *punt* the ball (kick it away) to the defense and give up possession.

The offense had success with the previous pass play, so needing 7 yards or more, you go for the pass. A successful 10-yard pass puts your team on the 48-yard line, and you get a new set of downs.

This continues until your team is unable to get another first down and must punt the ball, or you lose possession of the ball on a *fumble* or *interception*, or you score a touchdown or a field goal. Then your opponents are given the same opportunity.

The Chain Gang

One of the more unfortunate nicknames used in football is the *chain gang*. Just outside the boundary at all football games are three or four officials whose job is to keep track of the *down and distance* to the *line to gain*, the spot at which a first down is achieved. A chain exactly 10 yards in length is attached to two poles for measuring the distance to the point that is 10 yards ahead of the ball. A third pole with an indicator on top with numbers from one to four keeps track of the progress of the ball and the number of the down at hand. All of the terms associated with down and distance come from judgments made on the basis of the chain gang's accuracy. This judgment, however, is made by the officials, not the chain gang. Still, second and 6, third and 8, and fourth and inches are all educated guesses—except, of course, for first and 10.

reserved as a fourth-down maneuver, and once the ball crosses the line of scrimmage, possession goes to the receiving team.

Line of Scrimmage

At many points during a game, the ball will be spotted on the field and made ready for play by the officials. When this is done, an imaginary line is drawn from sideline to sideline through the front point of the ball (the point aimed at the defensive goal line). This is the *line of scrimmage* (LOS) and is the starting point for the down. After the down has ended, a new line of scrimmage is established that is the starting point for the next down.

Kicking

Besides the offensive plays and the defenses designed to stop them, coaches are equally concerned with the third phase of the sport: kicking. For all of the time spent on offensive play and defensive reactions, the biggest gains or losses, the longest plays, and the greatest opportunities to gain territory happen in this part of the sport. A *kick* is the intentional striking of the ball with the foot. The kicking game, as it is commonly referred to, is further divided into two types of kicking situations: free kicks and scrimmage kicks.

Free Kicks

The best-known free kick is the *kickoff*, the ritualized start of the football game. The kickoff is also used after a score and to start the second half of the game, and always takes place from a scrimmage line established specifically for restarting play. Kickoffs must come from the ground, with the ball being supported on a tee. The only time the ball may be kicked by holding it is after the defense has scored a *safety* by forcing the offense to down the ball in their own end zone. Then the ball can be kicked on the ground or out of the kicker's hand, which is called a punt.

Scrimmage Kick

A scrimmage kick, as it implies, happens as part of a scrimmage down. It can be used to score or can be a defensive maneuver to put your opponent farther away from a potential score. If it is used to score, it is called a field goal and is worth 3 points to the offense. A scrimmage kick is also a way to score a single point after a touchdown, often referred to as the *point after touchdown* (PAT) (see below) or *point after attempt*. In both cases, the ball must be kicked from the ground.

Punting the ball, the second type of scrimmage kick, occurs when the kicker holds the ball in his hands. Punting is a defensive play and attempts to push an opponent further from a scoring attempt. When you punt, you are giving up possession of the ball to the other team. If by some fluke your kicker's punt should go through the opponent's goal posts and over the crossbar (like it would for a successful field goal or a point after touchdown), it does *not* earn any points for your team. Rather, like any other punt that enters your opponent's end zone, the ball will be brought out and spotted on your opponent's 20-yard line and their offense will start from there.

The Scoring System

Touchdowns

If all goes well for the offense, it will advance the ball to the goal line. The front edge of the chalk is part of this line. Consequently, the entire line is in the end zone, so once the ball has "broken the vertical plane," that is, it's on or above the line and is in possession of an attacking player, a touchdown has been scored, and the offensive team receives 6 points.

Points after Touchdown (PAT)

Immediately after the touchdown, the scoring team has the opportunity to score additional points called, not surprisingly, the points after touchdown (PAT). This can be accomplished in two ways. The ball is spotted at the 3-yard line. In what is technically called a *try*, teams can elect two different types of strategies to score. The first is to use a regular scrimmage play to gain the 3 yards by running or passing the ball. If the scoring team chooses this method and is successful, it scores 2 points. The second way is to use a *scrimmage kick play*, or kicking the ball from the ground and through the goal posts above the crossbar. One point is awarded for kicking the PAT. However, at the youth level of football your league may want to adopt a reversal of scoring for the points after a touchdown, because kicking may be a greater accomplishment than running a scrimmage play. This would encourage place kicking at an earlier age.

Field Goals

Place kicking can also be used before the touchdown. We mentioned earlier that an option during a down was to choose to kick the ball. There are two different types of scrimmage kicks: a punt, where the ball is kicked while holding it in the air, and the *place kick*. If the team in possession of the ball elects the place kick, it is attempting to make a field goal. The same rules apply as for the PAT kicking attempt. If the field goal is successful, the team is awarded 3 points. If the field goal is missed, the ball is spotted on the defender's 20-yard line or at the spot from where the kick was attempted (whichever is farther from the defender's goal line), then the defense goes on offense from that spot.

Safeties and Touchbacks

The final method of scoring points in our game is called a *safety*. If, during a down, the defensive team traps the offensive team in their own end zone, and the down ends in the end zone, the defensive team scores a safety worth 2 points. The term is often confused with a *touchback*, which occurs when a team receiving a punt or kickoff is trapped in their end zone. The ball is put back in play at the receiving team's 20-yard line.

The Opposing Teams

Neither team can have more than eleven players on the field when the clock is running. Although it's strategically unsound, teams are not in violation of the rules if they have fewer players, but eleven is the limit.

The Offense

Offensive teams line up or align in what are called *formations*, which are alignments of players intended to best execute the type of play the team is using. Offensive formations are highly varied. Eleven factorial—the number of possible ways of arranging eleven objects—is an imposing figure, as all math whizzes can tell us. However, the rules of the game dictate specific restrictions. The length-of-the-football distance between the line of scrimmage and the back point of the ball is called the *neutral zone*. By rule, there must be at least seven players aligned motionless with the numbers of the jersey of the *center*, the player who is positioned over the ball and immediately behind the neutral zone. (Lining up in the neutral zone, or encroaching on it prior to the snap of the ball, is a foul.) In other words, if we drew a line through the numbers on the center's jersey from sideline to sideline, the offense would need to have at least six other players on that line who cannot move until the down begins. Moreover, five of these players need to have jerseys numbered 50 through 79 (local leagues may not enforce this rule). They can have more than seven players lined up, but six or fewer (including the center) would constitute an illegal formation. The four remaining

Offensive Positions (see diagram next page)

Center: Usually positioned in the center of the formation on the line, he is responsible for snapping or "centering" the ball to begin the play.

Flanker: A back who positions similarly to a split end and basically has the same duties.

Fullback: Usually the biggest and best blocking back, he is positioned right behind the quarterback and is best known as a lead blocker, pass protector, and short-yardage ball carrier.

Guard: A lineman usually positioned next to the center, who is the most mobile of the five interior linemen.

Halfback: Also referred to as a tailback, or running back. His job is to carry the ball, catch passes, and block for teammates in the running game.

Quarterback: Looked to for leadership, he has responsibility for the ball on every play. He can hand off, pass, or run himself. He is the communicator and the director on the field. All teams need good quarterbacks.

Slot back: A back positioned between a tackle and a split end. Serves the same purpose as a wing, but is in a better position to catch passes.

Split end: Positioned away from the interior linemen, but in business to catch passes and block the perimeter.

Tackle: Interestingly named, since it is illegal for offensive linemen to tackle, tackles are usually outside the guards and are noted for their strength and size.

Tight end: Positioned next to a tackle on the end of the line formation, tight ends are expected to block like an interior lineman and also catch passes.

Wing back: A back positioned next to a tight end to help establish a flanking position on the defense.

players have no alignment restrictions and can position themselves wherever the coach would like them. How and where these players align generally dictates the type of formation used.

The Defense

Defensive football teams have no rule restrictions on alignment, except they must be on their own side of the line of scrimmage. The eleven defensive players (see sidebar page 19) align in respect to defending the offense (see diagram next page); however, defenders are usually categorized into three position groups. *Defensive linemen* align near the line of scrimmage; they are the first line of defense and, loosely speaking, are responsible for defending the running plays. *Defensive backs* position themselves well off the line of scrimmage and are responsible for defending the flanks on runs and pass plays. The *linebackers* align between the "D-line" and "D-backs" and defend both runs and passes. How many are in each group depends on the style of defense employed and the tendencies and strength of the opposition.

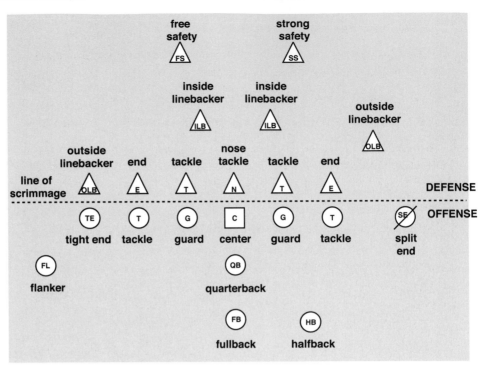

Typical offensive and defensive player alignment. Alignment positioning will change depending on what plays are run. (*Note:* this book uses triangles for defensive players and circles for offensive players; the center is always a square.)

We discuss more about defensive and offensive formations in chapters 4 and 5. The analogy that football is a human chess game is true: it's a game of specific players with specific roles and restricted movements.

Beginning a Game

One of the most misunderstood portions of the game is, oddly enough, the coin toss. This ritual has many strategic implications and can be a great tool in the hands of a wily tactician. There are four choices offered to the team that wins the toss. Most casual fans think that the winner receives the kick-off, the loser kicks, and the teams switch for the second half, but there's more to it. The winner of the toss chooses how to begin the game; the loser chooses how to begin the second half. Here's how it works.

Your captain calls "heads," and the coin comes up heads. There are four choices:

Receive: The opposing team kicks to you; it chooses what goal it wants to defend and, consequently, what direction it will kick.

Kick: You kick to the opposing team; it still can choose the goal to defend and the direction in which to kick (rarely used by coaches still employed).

Defend: You get to choose the goal you'll defend and the direction of the kick; the opposing team chooses to receive or kick (used when an extremely wet field or weather conditions favor the kicking game).

Defensive Positions

Cornerbacks (corners): Modern corners are primarily defensive backs who defend against the pass. A later arrival on running plays, corners defend the ball in the air.

End: A pass rusher and "containment" player positioned on the end of the defensive line.

Free safety: Similar to a strong safety, but aligns away from the strong safety.

Inside or middle linebackers: Hard-hitting and aggressive, these players are just in back of the defensive linemen, ready to search out and stop all running plays. They are the enforcers of the defense. They also are responsible for short pass attempts over the middle. Just as good offenses must have good QBs, all great defenses have great ILBs.

Outside linebacker: Part linebacker, part defensive back, OLBs are skilled and mobile and enjoy hard-hitting, open-field tackling.

Strong safety: These defensive backs are essentially outside linebackers with speed. Expected to be able to cover deep passes *and* attack the line of scrimmage, strong safeties need football intellect and great physical skills. This position usually attacks and defends the "strong side" of the offensive formation; that is, the side of the ball on which the majority of the offensive players line up for a play.

Tackle: Primarily responsible for an interior gap in the running game, a tackle is a down-stanced lineman who also is a pass rusher. If he is positioned nose to nose with the offensive center, he is called a "nose tackle" or "noseman."

Defer: You would rather have your choice at the start of the second half, so you give the opposing team the opportunity to choose now. Obviously, you'll need to prepare your captains well before they walk to the center of the field for their first coin toss.

After all the hands have been shaken and the choices made, the game begins with a kickoff. The kicking team aligns behind a yard line (the 40-yard line in the 6- to 12-year-old age group and high school, the 35 in college and the pros). The receiving team is at least 10 yards away in position to catch the kick. The referee whistles play to begin, the kicker kicks the ball to the receiving team, and play is underway. The receiving team advances the ball until tackled, the ball goes out-of-bounds, or they score. If a score does not happen, the first series of scrimmage downs begins as discussed earlier in this chapter. One point to note here is that after the ball has traveled 10 yards on the kickoff, it is a "free" ball, and either team can gain possession.

Length of the Game

To some of our colleagues in the more aerobic sports, discussions about the length of the game are a cause for some ribbing. Admittedly, there is down time in football, both literally and figuratively, but no one will argue that

Assigning Positions

You might be wondering just how you're supposed to figure out which child you should assign to play what position. Don't panic. It's likely that at least several of your players will have played the previous season and will already know how to play a position. However, that's not to say they haven't grown out of those positions.

Here's an example: Let's say last year little Sam was a quick and agile running back. This year, when you meet "little" Sam, you realize things have changed—last year's 60-pound 9-year-old is this year's 110-pound 10-year-old. Common sense alone would tell you not to keep "big" Sam as a running back, because not only might he hurt the 60-pound safety who tries to stop his run, but he'd also make a great lineman.

At this age level, it's important to size players up and match them accordingly. Within these size constraints, the best way to find positions for new players is to try them out at various ones and see what skills they have. Preparing your players to play at more than one position is not only advantageous, it might become a necessity. Have every new player throw, snap, kick, run, block, etc. By doing this and using a little common sense, you'll be able to position your kids where they are most comfortable. Many parents will want their child to be in a "glory" position, such as quarterback, running back, or receiver. Some of your players will want this too, but you'll quickly learn that not all of these players have the skills to fill those positions. You, as the coach, have the last word.

our busy time isn't action packed, exciting, and mentally and physically taxing.

Football is arranged into four quarters of playing time. Quarters for players under the age of 13 are usually 6 to 8 minutes in duration, with 10 minutes per quarter for middle school and high school freshmen games. Varsity and junior varsity high school quarters are 12 minutes, and college and professional games have 15-minute quarters. Varsity high school, college, and pro teams play various styles of overtime quarters in case of ties at the end of regulation, but overtime is not generally used in youth football leagues.

Basic Penalties

Violations of the rules of the game, in general, result in two types of penalties: live ball fouls and dead ball fouls. Infractions are generally penalized according to their effect on the game or the severity of illegal contact on opposing players. Penalties can happen before the down begins, during a down, or after a down has ended.

If the penalty happens before or after the down, the penalty is assessed automatically and is called a *dead ball foul.* However, if the foul occurs during a down or a free kick live ball, the offended team has the choice of taking the result of the yardage gains made during the down or the results of the penalty. These are *live ball fouls.* Some live ball penalties will include loss of down as a part of the assessment. Also, football is unique in that one foul—intentional grounding of a forward pass from within the end zone—actually scores 2 points for the defensive team (a safety).

Previous Spot and Succeeding Spot

In order to understand where penalties are assessed, the terms previous spot and succeeding spot are used. *Previous spot* simply means the spot where the ball was placed at the start of the down, and *succeeding spot* is the place where the ball ended up at the end of the down. Live ball fouls, depending on the infraction, are assessed as either being previous or succeeding spot fouls.

Penalties are assessed as 5-, 10-, or 15-yard penalties, with the exception that no penalty can bring the ball closer than half the distance to the goal line.

Common 5-Yard Penalties

Offside: The offense has lined up or moved into the neutral zone prior to the beginning of the down before the ball is snapped (dead ball foul).

Encroachment: The defense moves into the neutral zone prior the beginning of the down (dead ball foul).

False start: The offense, prior to the beginning of the down, makes a movement toward the line of scrimmage that resembles the start of a down (dead ball foul).

Illegal motion: Two offensive players move at the start of the down, or a back moves toward the line of scrimmage at the beginning of the down (live ball foul).

Illegal formation: The offense does not have seven players on the line of scrimmage (live ball foul).

Common 10-Yard Penalties

Holding: Keeping a player from advancing by holding him back. This is a live ball foul, and is the only common 10-yard penalty.

Common 15-Yard Penalties

Illegal personal contact: Roughing the passer, catcher, kicker, or holder, or unnecessary contact or roughness and fighting.

Illegal blocking: Blocking below the waist in certain situations, blocking in the back in all situations.

Illegal participation: Having twelve or more players on the field during a live ball.

Interference with ability to catch a kick or pass: Contact before the kick or pass arrives.

Noncontact unsportsmanlike acts: Improper actions or language toward opponents or officials including taunting (also includes disqualification).

Clipping: Blocking or hitting a player in the back other than the ball carrier.

Playing Safely

Every coach in every sport at every level has an unwavering responsibility for the physical and mental well-being of the players in their sport. Any time two objects are in motion, there is the possibility of collision and resulting injury. Not to be overlooked are the "esteem" injuries that can be just as devastating to a youngster as a strained ankle or a broken arm.

Football, by its nature, is the kind of activity that can build great self-worth in many different types of youngsters because of the variety of skills needed to make a team. Big ones, small ones, fast ones, athletically skilled ones, physically tough ones, and, most importantly, determined ones are all needed to make a team. The wise coach can see some contributing trait in each player and builds on those factors to generate enthusiasm and an individual sense of belonging for each player.

Sample Series of Downs: You Make the Call

Let's assume that your guys won the toss, and you have decided to receive. The result of the kickoff and return has brought the ball out to the 32-yard line on your side of midfield. Your return play took the ball between the left inbounds marker, also known as the *hash mark*, and the *boundary* (or sideline). The ball now is spotted on the left hash at the 32.

OK, Coach, what are you thinking? Well, it could be something like this:

It's first and 10. You've seen your opponent play before. You've observed that when the team is forced to defend the wide side of the field, it puts an extra defensive player to that side to compensate for the additional territory to be defended. Because of this tendency, you decide to put an extra person on the opposite (short) side of your formation, to attempt a flanking play to that side. Your strategy pays off as your runner gains 7 yards.

It's now second and 3, and you've created some options for your team. Given the fact that you've established your willingness to attack the short side, you could do it again. However, the opposing coach may make an adjustment and match your formation man for man, and with the additional advantage of the smaller area to cover he may outman you. Additionally, you may want to attempt a pass and go for big yardage; after all, you can always pick up the 3 yards needed to continue the possession on third down. However, you're at your own 39-yard line and not willing to take the risk of an unsuccessful passing play. You decide that the shortest distance between two points is a straight line, so you attempt a running play in the middle of the line. This time your opponent has loaded the middle and stops the run. Result: you're still at the 39-yard line.

It's now third and 3, a critical early point in the contest. Not making the line to gain on this down will probably mean a scrimmage kick on the

Keep Your Head Up!

All coaches should impress upon their players that their helmets are for protection, not a license for using the head in contact. "Keep your head up and make contact with your hands and shoulders" is a coaching rule that cannot be said too many times at practices, meetings, and games. "Putting your head between the numbers" may be great TV commentary, but it's extremely dangerous talk. For the offensive player, hitting head-first can result in a broken neck or broken spine. For the defensive player, tackling a player coming at them head-first can result in cracked ribs and other serious injuries. *It cannot be tolerated for the good of the game and the safety of the players.* This is the most important concept to teach your young players.

fourth down. Going three and out on your first possession is not a good way to build offensive confidence and instill fear in the defense, so this call is important. You decide that the wide side of the field is just too inviting. You match the other coach's overloading on the field by putting an extra player in a blocking position to the wide side. You have your team fake a running play up the middle to keep defenders occupied in that area, and you follow up with a flanking attack to the wide side. Good move, Coach, it's a 5-yard gain and a new set of downs.

You have used your knowledge of your opponent, a variety of actions, and wise field strategy to maintain possession. Your kids are developing team confidence, and your opponents know they're in for a tough game. We'll go over more of these plays and scenarios in chapter 8.

CHAPTER 3

Setting Up the Season

Football presents a unique athletic test of skill, speed, strength, intellect, and courage for the youngsters who choose to play it. It is also a sport involving a variety of talents that may have little in common with each other. While passing, catching, and ball skills are important to some players, they are less so to others. The differentiation of skill by position or groups of positions means that coaching the squad by yourself is not only difficult but nearly impossible. Many football novices make light of the number of assistants used by football programs. Although you may not need coordinators and coaches at each position, you will need at least two other people to assist you. This is a great time to get to know your local high school coach. Believe us, he will be a great source of help and information. Besides the obvious reasons for befriending him—you are working with his future players, after all—football coaches love to talk football. This will be especially helpful for the next phase of the job: organization.

Getting Help (aka Volunteers)

You are going to need help with the team; someone with a background in the sport is certainly a plus. There may be other parents like yourself who are willing to get involved. Call people you know first, whether or not they have kids on the team—it's often better if they don't! Recent graduates of your local high school can be good assistants, and their former coach will know if their temperament and maturity would work in your situation. The bottom line is you will need help. It's always important to remember that, like you, these people are volunteering their time.

On most teams at this level, the kids play on both offense and defense, or on "both sides of the ball." Defensive football is broken down into three groups of related players: the linemen, linebackers, and the secondary. We suggest that you, as head coach, work directly with the linebackers and that you have help from at least two assistant coaches to work with the linemen and the secondary. This will allow you to see the two other groups because at some point in your practice the linebackers should practice with them.

For the offense, you'll need at least one assistant to coach the group you don't: either the offensive line or the backs. Unless you have lineman-playing experience, you should choose to coach the backs. This will give you a working relationship with the primary team communicators, the quarterbacks. Your second assistant can either assist you with the backs or coach receivers.

How you assign duties to your volunteer assistants will depend mostly on what you want to accomplish and their knowledge and experience. The important thing here is that everyone have a firm understanding of their roles. You and your assistants will need to have meetings to define roles for a harmonious working relationship and also to formulate a playbook for both sides of the ball and the kicking game. In addition, practice schedules and responsibilities at practice must be clearly understood by each coach so that workouts will run smoothly. It's not overkill to formulate job descriptions for each coach and to delegate coaching and administrative duties. As head coach, you shouldn't burden yourself with every little detail. Nevertheless, details need to be attended to. It's poor coaching organization to have your players standing around because some piece of the teaching tools is not on the field. Dividing the details among coaches makes it less likely that something will be forgotten. Part of being head coach is to delegate duties, and part of being an assistant is to make your job go more efficiently.

Unite as Coaches

It's important that the players see that the coaches respect one another. It's even more important that the players believe the coaches are always in complete accord in relation to the operation of the team. *Never show anything but a united front!* This has to be stressed in coaching meetings from the outset. The team needs to be a unit, and nothing will cause division in your team like a public disagreement between coaches. You're the one in charge, and if you need to correct an assistant, do so out of earshot of the players. You'll undermine your coach's position with his group and the team by open criticism. Conversely, an assistant should always show loyalty to you in front of the team. This is not to say that you and your assistants will always agree about plays and personnel. All football staffs have differing opinions, and some discussions can become heated, but they should never be in front of players or other parents. Staff meetings, formal and informal, are the places for all to express opinions, discuss them, and make decisions in the best interests of the kids. When decisions are made, each coach needs to accept what is final and move on. Therefore, in the eyes of the

Equipment

Players (each piece of equipment should be labeled with the player's name)

football helmet

shoulder pads

girdle pads

thigh pads

knee pads

white pants (practice)

practice shirt

game shirt

game pants

shoes (most kids use soccer-style shoes with molded cleats; no sneakers or metal cleats!)

socks

water bottle

mouth guard

athletic supporter (optional)

A fully equipped player. His coach is checking his mouth guard.

The coach checking the chin-strap connection. Properly fitting equipment is essential, especially when it comes to safety.

Coaches

footballs (youth size—used for players up through 8th grade)

pinnies/scrimmage vests

whistles

kicking tees

blocking dummies (optional)

blocking shields

cones

chalkboard/chalk

basic first-aid kit

cell phone

Most leagues provide the helmets, pads, shirts, and pants; players are responsible for maintaining those items during the season. Players also must provide their own water bottles, mouth guards, shoes, socks, and, if desired, athletic supporter. In addition to protective gear for every single player on your squad, you'll need footballs, and more than you think. Between the various groups and individual drills you'll be running, a minimum of nine balls will be needed to run an effective workout. Each coach will need a whistle to control the drill and to get your players accustomed to stopping when the whistle is sounded. You'll need a dozen or so scrimmage vests—what P.E. teachers call "pinnies"—to separate teams and groups.

players, you're all on the same page. Ultimately, this will strengthen the fabric of the group and make for a more cohesive unit.

The Big Picture

Success in this sport is dependent on how well you prepare your team. That may sound obvious, but although some team sports can ride on the talents of a few outstanding individuals, football can't. Individuals can display their gifts only if the team's play allows them to perform. The entire group needs to be prepared, or the stars won't shine—no matter how talented they may be.

Preparation for the season has two distinct phases: preseason camp and regular season. Each has different goals, but most coaches will tell you that without an organized and effective preseason, the rest of the campaign will be uphill. The key is to spend time before the season begins and be organized from the very first minute you step on to the practice field.

Plan Ahead: Preseason Camp

In formulating your plans, you should start with the date of your first game and work backward to the date of your first practice. Remember, you're preparing to be ready to play opening day. This means that the bulk of your offensive and defensive thinking needs to be in place and operating for the first contest. Don't forget the third phase of the sport, the kicking game, as all phases of that will need to be in place so your team will be prepared for success on opening day. In football lingo, this is preseason camp or just "camp." This time is basic training for a football team.

To illustrate what we mean, let's say you have two weeks with your team before your first contest, and you're going to have practice each weeknight and on Saturday morning. That means you'll have twelve workouts with the kids. The last practice before each game is usually reserved for a run-through—sort of a dress rehearsal. It will be a limited teaching day, so we won't include this practice in our teaching plans for your camp. For the practices that will be the bulk of your preseason, you'll need to install your offensive and defensive formations and alignments and put in all phases of the kicking game. It's probably a good idea, at least initially in fundamental and group work, to have some offensive and some defensive skills in each practice.

Overplan for Practices

Deciding how much to include in each practice will be one of your tasks as head coach. It's a good idea to overplan and then cut back if necessary. What you don't accomplish in the first practice can be included in the next. It's critical that you keep your offensive schemes related so that your players can associate one play's relationship to the next. This could take the form of teaching plays in sequence, such as a power off-tackle play, followed by a power sweep and then a play-action pass off the same backfield maneuver. Or maybe teaching a variety of sweep plays in the same practice; any gimmick that will help your players remember. Don't give your players too much at once, and remember, repetition is the key to consistent execution. So allow plenty of time for your players to repeat what they're being shown both in their own group and as a unit. You'll find that offense takes longer to instill than defense. Because of this, some coaches think that they can sacrifice defensive time and spend more time on their offensive plans. Your defense may be ahead of your offense, but it should receive equal practice time, or those critical skills will be lost—and so, too, your next game.

Add New but Repeat the Old

Plan to add new material at each practice during your camp, but make sure you have time to repeat the old material as well. Don't be overly concerned with perfection in the beginning. As you add new plays and drills and allow for repetition, repetition, and more repetition, mastery will come. If your plans are sound and you stick to them, your team will progress as a unit. Try to divide your plan into the number of practices that you're going to have in your preseason. The "big picture" should be the end product of the puzzle pieces you're putting together with your staff and your players. Like any puzzle, it starts as a complete picture—your plan for the kids in your charge—now broken into parts but to be put together in a joint team effort by all concerned with the success of your team.

After each practice evaluate your plan and your work. Not everything will flow as you'd envisioned; as a matter of fact, you can count on variations. Assess what you've done, reinforce the positive aspects, and give the negatives one more shot. If it works, use it; if it doesn't, drop it.

The Kicking Game, Again

As important as the two other phases, the kicking game should be presented and practiced the first time your team meets. Generally, we can categorize kicking into three sets of offensive and defensive teams: punt and punt return, kickoff and kickoff return, and point after touchdown and field goals. The latter two groups, especially field goals, may be a stretch with younger kids, but you'll be the talk of your league if you win one game 3 to 0. It might be worth a look in a prepractice period to see if your team has any talent in this area, but if not, don't practice it. If kicking the point after touchdown also is not going to be a part of your game plan, take this period of time to master what plays you plan to use to score those all-important extra points. The other parts of the kicking game will definitely need to be mastered before your first game. In the beginning, do one each practice: punt on Monday, punt return on Tuesday, and so on. Practice this with all of your kids and give them specific assignments in this phase. Don't just have them fill in spots. After you've chosen your special teams, then practice two of them together at each practice.

As the preseason camp ends and the first game approaches, the big picture should start to resemble a football team. The focus of your practices now switches from introduction to practical application. The word *focus* is an apt description of what these practices are all about. For the remainder of the season, each workout will be directed toward schemes and maneuvers to outwit and outhit the opposition. If you've done a good job in preseason camp, you will draw from those often-repeated and now-mastered skills you worked on from day one. In preparing your team for the game, your game plan will concentrate on plays and defenses that will give your team the opportunity to win. You may add a special wrinkle or gadget from time to time, but what you use on game day is what you worked on in camp. You won't use all the plays you practice in every game, but you should pick and choose the ones that will work against the opposing team. Now you should be concerned with perfect play execution, and you should practice for perfection.

We have purposely put preseason preparation first because we firmly believe that before you contact players and parents, fit equipment, and hand out uniforms, you need to thoroughly plan all of the above and think it through.

Preseason Meeting

This initial meeting with your players needs to include their parents, and we recommend that it not be part of a practice session. Whether you have a picnic or just a get-together, its purpose should be informational in nature. Divide up the players' names among your assistants and call each family with information on the place and date of your initial meeting. Explain the purpose, and make it mandatory that at least one parent be present. Follow up this call with a postcard or a short letter (see sidebar next page).

At the meeting, introduce yourself and your assistants and describe what phase of the game they will be coaching. Briefly explain your philosophy and your expectations. This needs to be made part of a document that you distribute to each player and his family to post on the refrigerator or somewhere prominent. Speeches can be forgotten, and remembered statements can be misinterpreted, but the written word is exact in its content.

Player behavior toward teammates, coaches, officials, and opponents should be clearly a part of any statement of expectations. Parents, too, should be made aware of their role in making certain that the experience is rewarding for their child. We recommend that you be up-front and explicit concerning the handling of parents' complaints and concerns. Make it clear that all discussions will be limited to their child only, and that discussions of

Sample Preseason Letter to Parents

Dear Parents:

Another football season is upon us. I'm excited about our team and hope your kids are, too.

My primary goal for the season is for everyone to have fun and improve their football skills. My basic philosophy is to foster a positive, supportive atmosphere so that every player has a great experience. Regardless of ability, every member of the team deserves to be treated with encouragement. Players should respect each other on and off the field and should learn both to win and lose well. I look to you to help reinforce these important concepts: when you come to games or practices, please limit your interaction with your children to positive encouragement from a distance. During games, please treat the officials with the respect they deserve. We are our children's most important role models. I'll set as good an example as I possibly can, and I would greatly appreciate your help by doing the same.

Games: Please make every effort to arrive at games 30 minutes before the scheduled start. If you know that getting your child to a game will be difficult, we can carpool. If your child can't make it to a game, please let me know in advance. If he misses practice the week before the game without a good reason, he might not play in the game. Please know that I have this policy so that participation in the games is fair to everyone.

Cancellation: Unless you hear otherwise, we'll always have practice or games. In the case of cancellation, kids will be notified either at school or by means of the enclosed phone tree.

Must bring: Please make sure that your child has his helmet, pads, practice uniform, appropriate shoes, and a water bottle. These, and other personal equipment, should be labeled with your child's name.

We're looking forward to a great season of football. If you have any questions or concerns, please feel free to contact me.

Thanks,
The Coach
526 Hill Street
555-1234
coach@football.com

players other than their own is off limits. This will reassure parents that issues of comparison of players' abilities are limited to the coaching staff. Parents will appreciate that you won't be talking about their children with other parents.

Another important point in dealing with parental concerns or complaints is to never allow discussion to be in front of the players. This is vital. You should be available often and in many places, but in the presence of the child is not one of them. Again, we feel parents will appreciate your motives for this when they have the time to think through its reasoning.

Fitting Equipment

The preseason meeting is an excellent time to issue equipment. As we stated on pages 9–10, make sure you have expert help or have been instructed in the proper fitting of protective gear. This is not only for the best protection of your players, but for your legal protection, too. Helmets and shoulder pads absolutely need to be properly fitted to the athlete to maximize their effectiveness. Conversely, improper fit can actually be dangerous, adding to the risk to your players. Remember, football at this age is relatively safe. This is not to understate the possibility of an injury. Although rare, catastrophic injuries—including death—have occurred over the years. Rule changes and advances in protective equipment have greatly reduced the number of serious injuries, but the equipment can't do its work without proper fit. Make sure you have all the information you need to do the best job possible in this area. Of all the information you'll read about in this book, this is the most important.

Well, Coach, you've held your preseason meeting, handed out your rules and regulations, met with your parents, established guidelines and parameters with them, and equipped your team. It's now time to get your players ready to compete.

Questions and Answers

Q. My team roster has twenty-four names on it. Is that too many?

A. No, not at all; the more the merrier! Football has twenty-two starting positions, without specialists. Most high school coaches begin to worry if their roster has less than forty players. Even with twenty-four, we would keep recruiting. As you'll learn, you will want multiple players assigned to each position in case a child is hurt, tired, or is being substituted by another player. On game day, you'll refer to *depth charts* (see pages 84–86) that have at least two players at each position. Again, this will all depend on the size of your league. You might find that you barely have enough players to fill all twenty-two starting positions. If that's the case, some of your kids will be playing both offense and defense—or "both sides of the ball."

Q. What should I know about playing shoes?

A. Your leagues should have rules. Don't let anyone practice with hard, metal-tipped, or baseball-type spikes. Sneakers are not a good idea, either. Soccer-style shoes with molded cleats will work just fine. Check the shoes, however, so that no one gets a cut hand when stepped on.

Q. When I see football practices on TV and at my local high school, I see blocking dummies and sleds and apparatuses like that. Do I need them?

A. If you have access to such equipment, they can be good tools, but if you don't have access, you can run a very effective workout without them. The drills in this book are designed to use a one-on-one, light-contact approach with or without the use of hitting bags and sleds.

Q. I'm not good with names. How will I remember all those names?

A. Put some athletic tape on the front of each helmet before you issue them to your team. Have each kid (or a parent) print his name on the tape. Also, make an effort to greet the players by name at practices. After the first few practices, you should be able to remember most names. If not, the tape on the helmets will help.

CHAPTER 4

Essential Skills: Defensive Football

This chapter will go over the fundamentals of defensive football. From basic formations, defending the run, defending the pass, to proper tackling techniques and more, you'll be introduced to the skills your players need to start the season. For the novice coach, an understanding of defensive structure will make offensive strategies easier to see. Furthermore, strong defensive skills are crucial to your team's success. This information, combined with the drills in chapter 10, will help you get started and get your defense working toward game day. Teach these skills and alignments selectively according to the ages of your players. Concepts of gap coverage and alignment techniques will make more sense to 12-year-olds than to 6-year-olds. Use your judgment.

The Mission

The job of your defense is to prevent the opponent from scoring. How this is accomplished goes back to what we discussed about the rules of the game in chapter 2. Remember, the offense needs to go 10 yards in four plays in order to maintain possession of the ball. So if your defense can keep the offense under 2.5 yards per down, the offense will lose the ball. Job accomplished for the defense. This is assuming that the offense is willing to use all four downs to attempt to get the necessary yardage to keep the ball. Often the offense will be unwilling to risk losing the ball without some gain in territory and will take the final down to punt the ball away. In this case the defense has an easier job; if you keep the offense under 3.3 yards per down, you'll have a successful series. How the offense will use its downs generally depends on how much field position will be gained by punting and how close the offense is to scoring. The terms three-down territory, four-down territory, and red zone relate to offensive field position, and these zones on the field are shown in the diagram next page. In *three-down territory*, the offense is likely to punt the ball on fourth down. It would be too risky to go for the

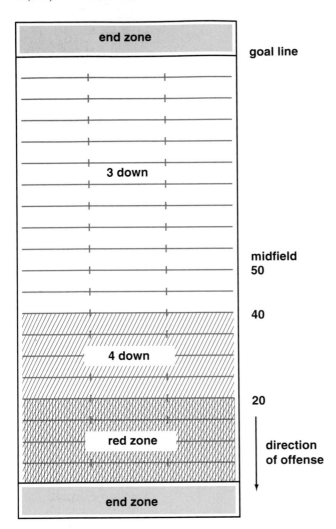

In three-down territory, the offense plays to punt on the fourth down. In other words, the risk of giving up the ball deep in its own territory is too great to accept. In four-down territory, an offense reasonably can risk trying to get a first down on fourth down. If your offense is in the red zone, you should use all four downs to try to score. Attempt a field goal on fourth down if your team has a good kicking game. Otherwise, go for a first down or touchdown.

first down because if the offense doesn't get it, your defense would get the ball with good field position relative to your opponent's end zone. If the offense is in *four-down territory*, they might go for a first down instead of punting. Even if the offense isn't successful, turning the ball over to the defense in this area of the field would strategically be OK. The *red zone* is scoring territory; the offense will use all four downs to try to score.

This thinking, however, is thrown out the window by the breakaway run or the long pass—the "big play." Staying away from the big play, keeping the offense out of four-down territory, and holding the offense to short gains is sound defensive thinking.

The diagrammed limits of three- and four-down territory are only a guide. A coach's willingness to gamble on offense will vary with personality, personnel, and situation. Late in the game with your team trailing, the whole field may be four-down territory.

Tendencies

Offensive football presents two separate challenges to defensive teams: a running game and a passing game. Defensive structure is designed to stop both, but various defensive schemes have better success at one phase than the other. If you're confident that your opponent is only going to run, it's best to position your players near the line of scrimmage. If they will most likely run *and* have no speed threat, you could position your defense on the line of scrimmage and toward the middle of the formation. Although most offensive teams have their signature tendencies, they all have the ability to run in a variety of locations and to pass at least enough to keep your defense from putting eleven players within 5 yards of the line of scrimmage.

Tendencies also involve down and distance. Some situations lend themselves to predictability. If it's third and 20, it's sound defensive thinking to assume that your opponent is going to use a different play than if it's third and 1. Although there are no absolutes, a wise coach observes and adjusts to these factors.

Defending the Offense

Skills aside for the present, let's examine some general principles. In doing this, we'll identify an area to defend and assign personnel to those responsibilities.

Offensive running plays can be categorized with respect to the location they're attacking relative to offensive linemen. *Interior running plays* are defined as attacking at the center position and the two guards next to him. *Off-tackle plays* attempt to run at the tackle position or just inside the tight end. *Sweep plays* are wide plays toward the perimeter, outside the offensive line set.

In defending these points of attack, let's examine the offensive line. The space between adjacent offensive linemen is called a *gap*. Offenses attack gaps. If the offensive line uses a tight end, it will present the defense with seven gaps to defend. If the offense decides to play with two tight ends,

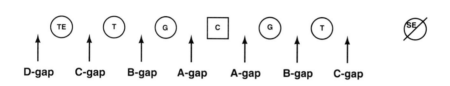

The space between offensive linemen is called a *gap*. Your defense will learn to recognize and defend these gaps, also known as seams.

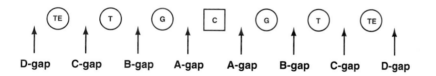

Starting with the center, each gap is given a letter, A through D, out toward the flanks on both sides. Defending these gaps is called *gap control*.

then the defense will have an additional gap to defend (see the diagrams).

Each gap is given a letter, starting from the center and working out toward the flanks, right and left, A through D. Each of these seams, or gaps, needs to be defended, and assigning positions to these gaps is called *gap control*. Let's look at two defenses and how they defend these gaps.

Eight-Front Even Defense

In football terms, an *even defense* has an even number of linemen. The *front* refers to the total number of linemen and linebackers. An eight-front even defense is called a 4-4 because the front is divided into four linemen and four linebackers. This defense is also called "Eight in the Box," the box being the area within 4 yards of the line of scrimmage and between the tight ends. Putting the eighth player in the front means you are defending the run; hence, "Nothing stops the run like . . ."

An eight-man defensive front. Nothing stops the run like "Eight in the Box," the saying goes.

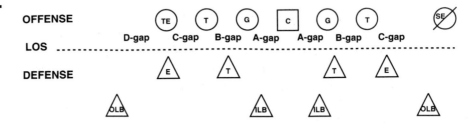

In this set, the two defensive tackles (T) are B-gap responsible, and the defensive end (E) on the three-lineman side is assigned C-gap, while the right defensive end has flank responsibility because there is no tight end on his side. The outside linebacker (OLB) on the three-lineman side is the flank defender, while the outside linebacker on the two-lineman side can fill inside his defensive end if the point of attack by the offense is on his side, or he can check for any counters or cutback plays going away from him. The inside linebackers (ILB) are initially A-gap players, but if those areas are not threatened, they can flow to the ball.

As you can see, an eight-front defense with seven gaps to defend gives the defense a numerical advantage at the line of scrimmage. This is good, especially if you're defending against a run. Missing from the diagram are the positions of the defensive backs (see pages 17 and 18). With only three players left in the secondary, this group can be easily stretched thin by wide positioning of receivers and running backs. This is not a good situation, especially against a good passer and speedy receivers.

Seven-Front Odd Defense

A seven-front odd defense has an odd number of defensive linemen, for a total of seven when combined with the linebackers. The particular model diagrammed here is called the Oklahoma 5-2. It was developed at the University of Oklahoma and has evolved into many different and effective defenses.

In this scheme, a large portion of what is to be done will depend on the match between the noseman or nose tackle (N) and the offensive center (C). If the nose tackle can handle the center, we may make him a two-gap

This seven-front odd defense has five defensive linemen and two linebackers for a total of seven (as compared to the eight-front even defense where there are four linemen and four linebackers). Lined up behind them in the secondary are the two corners and the two safeties.

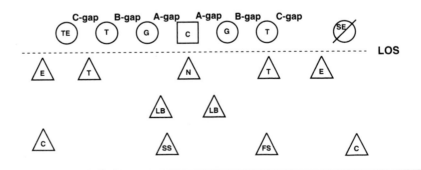

player and assign him the A-gap on both sides. This gives us all the advantage of the eight-front defense with seven players. It may also force the offense to use an adjacent offensive lineman to block the nose tackle, another plus. However, if the center is a better player, the defense will lose its numerical advantage, having seven players for seven gaps. Additionally, if the offense now decides to play with two tight ends, this will give the defense another gap to defend: seven against eight, advantage offense.

Let's allow, though, for at least a statistical standoff to continue the discussion. If we slant the defense toward the three-side, the end is a flank defender, the tackle is filling the C-gap, the nose tackle is responsible for the A-gap to the three-man side of the offense. On the two-man side the tackle is filling the B-gap, and the end is the flank defender.

The two linebackers (LB) are flow players. The three-side linebacker (the tight-end side) has the B-gap if flow is his way, and he has the A-gap on the two-side if the ball goes away from him. His partner has the A-gap and also can fill inside the defensive end on his side.

Because this scheme has four players in the secondary, wide offensive sets are not as significant an alignment challenge as when you're an eight-front team. These players can also be brought into the front when additional seams are presented by the offense so the advantage we talked about when confronted with two tight ends can be matched, at least numerically. Remember, Coach: nothing stops the run like "Eight in the Box."

Three-Man versus Four-Man Secondary

A seven-front defense can quickly become an eight-front defense by bringing a secondary player up to the line of scrimmage. Let's look at both forms of secondary for strengths and weaknesses and determine how they might be utilized at your level. The role of the defensive backs demands that you have players with advanced athletic skills. They have to defend the ball when the offense is passing and be prepared to be primary defenders on *perimeter plays* (plays that go around the outside of the formation and toward the sidelines) as well. Mistakes by defensive backs usually result in

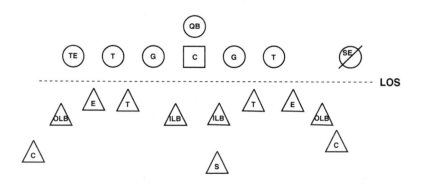

Eight-front, three-deep, #1: A typical three-deep secondary that includes two corners (C) and a safety (S). The eight-front defends the run, and the three players in the secondary defend against the pass.

those big plays we are trying to avoid. They need to be "sure" players: sure tacklers, sure-handed, and sure of their assignments.

Some eight-front coaches simply let the front defend the running plays of the offense and let the defensive backs cover passes. If the defensive backs get to the line of scrimmage to help defend the run, that's a bonus. Otherwise, you're giving a numerical advantage on a running play to the offensive team. To avoid this, you may want to rotate your three-deep scheme to a two-deep arrangement after the down begins, depending on the movement of the ball (see illustration). This is strong to a lone tight-end side, but it can be problematic to a split-end side as the acting safety may have difficulty catching up to a split receiver from his rotated position. There is much to like in this arrangement, however, especially if the run is your primary concern.

Eight-front, three-deep, #2: To help defend against a running play by the offense, you can rotate your three-deep scheme to a two-deep arrangement *after* the down begins. This is a great arrangement if you're playing an offense that primarily runs the ball.

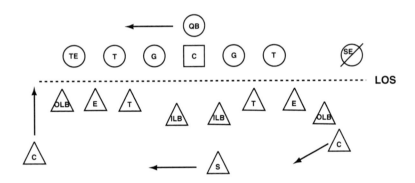

A four-man secondary has greater flexibility than a three-deep secondary. As stated earlier, it can easily become an eight-front by rotation, before or after the down begins.

The basic four-man secondary: two corners and two safeties. This is a very flexible formation that can quickly become a three-deep or even a two-deep formation depending on what play the offense runs. (Linemen and linebackers not shown.)

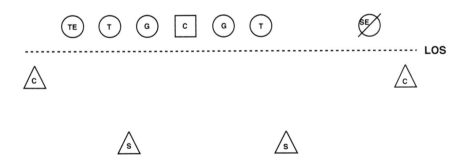

Four-Deep Alignment Rotated to Three-Deep

This type of maneuver is strong to the split-end side, as the defender aligned on the split end can keep good position on him without having to worry about short or "underneath" coverage. This is what coaches call *leverage.*

You can even rotate to both sides on the same play so both cornerbacks will be in position near the line of scrimmage. This will leave you with only the safeties in a deep position.

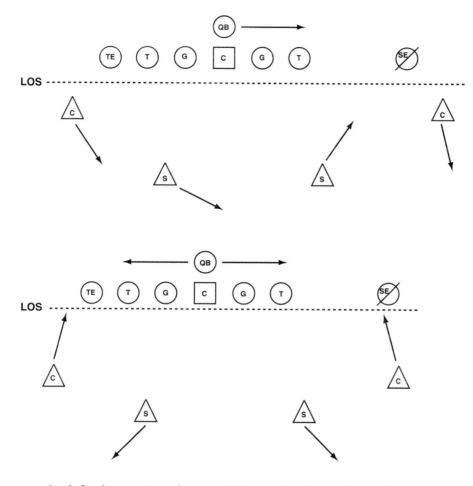

Rotating from four-deep to three-deep: As the QB moves the ball to the split-end side, the four-deep secondary rotates accordingly, with one going to the LOS and the other three defending the pass.

The "double zone" defensive alignment moves both cornerbacks to the line of scrimmage to defend the run, but leaves only two safeties to defend against deep passes. If your players are very young, you won't have to worry about a deep passing threat.

In defending against the run, defensive backs are *force players*, meaning they are going to force the perimeter runner to go in one direction. The direction toward which to force the runner depends on how you want to secure the flank. Some coaches want their force players to contain the ball carrier and force him into the ten other defenders in pursuit. Others want the ball carrier to bounce deeper and be forced into the sideline. Both of these are sound practices.

Defending against the Thrown Ball

Five offensive players are eligible to catch a forward pass, excluding the thrower. They are easily identified by having jerseys numbered between 1 and 49 or between 80 and 99. Unless your league has an unusual local rule, these are the only players who can be receivers. Defensive teams generally try to prevent these five offensive players from being effective by using *zone* or *man-to-man defense*.

Zone Defense

In its purest form, zone defenders, after recognizing that a pass is coming, go to a predetermined spot and defend an area of the field. The advantage is that your player doesn't necessarily have to be quicker or more skilled than the players he's matched against because he is defending territory, not a player. If done properly, it works.

If you decide to cover with a zone defense, you'll need to establish how best to blanket the field with your players. In a normal situation, you'll have seven players at your disposal to get the job done. These players are the linebackers and the defensive backs.

Start with the deep zones and decide how many you need based on the personnel you're playing against and the down and distance you need to defend. Usually this means either two or three deep zones, each beginning about 12 yards off the line of scrimmage. Give the zones an equal width and assign a defender to each of these deep areas. Tell your defenders to stay deeper than any of the opposing players, to *always watch the quarterback throw the ball*, and to go catch (and intercept) it.

Between the deep zones and the line of scrimmage are the *under*

> If you decide to play zone defense, and are playing with a three-deep secondary, you'll have three deep zones for the secondary and four under zones that would be covered by your linebackers. A big shortcoming of this type of defense is that now there are only four players left to rush the quarterback.

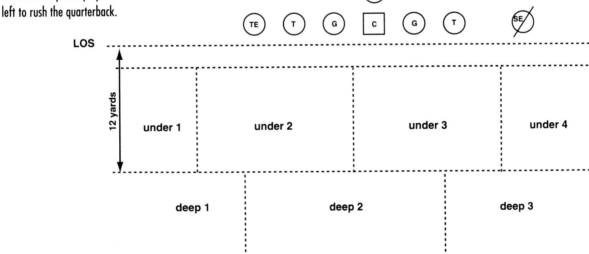

zones. If you're playing three-deep, you have four under zones; with two-deep, you have five under zones. In basic form, the same principles apply: divide up the area and assign players to those areas when the offense is passing. The biggest shortcoming of zone defense is that there are now only four players left to rush the passer.

Another problem is that all passes call for the same response from zone defenders. Whether there are five receivers in the pattern or only one, you've committed seven people to defend areas of the field, and they may be the only ones who show up in those areas. This is a big waste of manpower.

Man-to-Man Defense

Man-to-man defense is just as simple as zone defense, and maybe even easier. Look at the opposition's formation and start to number eligibles from the outside in. Now examine your defense in the same way. Have your number 1s assigned to your opponent's number 1s, 2s to 2s, and 3s to 3s. Tell your players that if the opposing player runs a pass route, they should cover the opponent, and if the opposing player blocks, then look for the run. If you're worried about someone being overmatched, don't assign one of your safeties to anyone. He can be free to roam center field. This is a simple defense, and lots of coaches do it. Its problems begin with perimeter defense: if an offensive player looks like he's running a pass route, he can take your primary sweep defender on a wild goose chase. This is a big waste of manpower.

Other Defense Considerations

Football is full of special situations. Defenses need to be set up for the goal line, short yardage other than the goal line, long yardage, and the end of the half or game. You may want to stay close to your normal structure, and that's OK. The caution here is that you'll need to think about these special situations and consider the problems they invariably present.

Teaching Defensive Skills and Drills

Unlike offensive players, who know where the ball is going to go on each play as soon as they leave the huddle, defensive players don't know where the ball is going until the offense tells them by their actions. How quickly your team recognizes and interprets those offensive moves will determine their success as a defensive unit. Although at times defensive teams look helter-skelter, good teams execute their assignments in an orderly, progressive fashion. No matter what style or structure of defense you decide on, your players will all need to be taught in a sequential progression, without skipping steps.

The Steps to Good Defense

We teach our defense in five steps. Each step must be completed as rapidly as possible, especially after the down has started. Once one step is accomplished, the players move along the progression to the next step. The five steps are as follows:

1. Alignment and stance
2. Initial
3. Recognize and react
4. Pursuit
5. Tackle or intercept

Step 1: Alignment and Stance

How to Align the Defensive Line

We've already set up a system of gap responsibility (see pages 35–39) so that our players can understand their first area to defend. Now we establish a similar procedure to ensure we can communicate proper alignment to our defensive front.

Again, let's use the offensive linemen as points of reference in establishing defensive locations, alignments, and techniques. Different coaches use different codes, but we suggest an easy system to ensure your defensive linemen are in the most advantageous position.

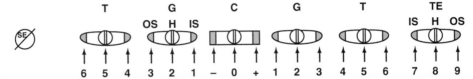

Alignment numbers: By assigning imaginary numbers to the shoulders and heads of the players on the offensive line, you can signal your defense what stance to take.

OS: outside shoulder
H: head on
IS: inside shoulder

For our purposes, let's establish that 1, 4, and 7 are inside-shoulder alignment techniques, and 3, 6, and 9 are outside-shoulder techniques. Using your player's nose as an aiming point, the number tells him where to take his stance. We could further refine this by adding an "I" to the number for inside eye or outside eye adjustments. An inside eye alignment is between straight on and the opponent's inside shoulder. An outside eye alignment is simply the opposite. Numbers 0, 2, 5, and 8 are head-up alignments. The + and − techniques on the center are shoulder alignments unless an adjustment word is used. Thus, a 5-technique defensive tackle would line up nose to nose with an offensive tackle. A 9-technique defensive end would align with the outside shoulder of the tight end. And an I-3 tackle would line up against the outside eye of the opposing guard.

Let's apply this to the two defenses described earlier in this chapter (see pages 35–37). In the version of an even eight-front defense shown, there are, in your base form, two 3-technique tackles and two 7-technique defensive ends. Because you were defending a split end and had no tight end on that side on which to align, your defensive end on the split side needs to imagine a tight end and align as if he were there, on his "ghost."

This "ghost" alignment applies to our seven-front sample defense as well. In that defense, you have a "9" defensive end, a "6" defensive tackle, and a "0" technique nose tackle. This system allows you to quickly communicate alignments to your defensive linemen and permits quick correction and easy adjustments.

How to Align the Linebackers

Inside linebackers (ILB) can use the same system to establish proper position. The difference, of course, is that linebackers are 3 to 4 yards off the line of scrimmage. In both sample defenses the inside linebackers are in a "2" (head-on) alignment.

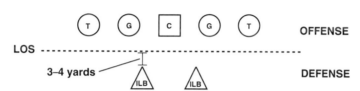

The inside linebackers use the same numbering system for their proper positioning. The only difference is that they are 3 to 4 yards behind the line of scrimmage.

Outside linebackers (OLB) align relative to the positions of the players who are threatening. Because linebackers have responsibilities for defending against both the run and the pass, they need to vary their alignment depending on the location of potential receivers and the down and distance. Additionally, the location of the defensive backs also influences linebackers' alignment.

Only our even-front (eight-front) example illustrates outside linebackers. Notice that the linebacker on the tight-end side is relatively close to the line of scrimmage. The linebacker can afford to do this because the tight end is a close threat. A split end presents a wider threat, so the linebacker must loosen his alignment and move out away from the line of scrimmage.

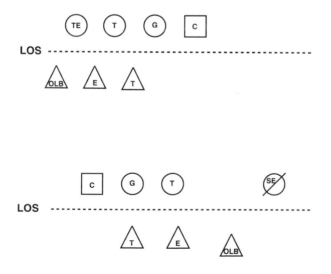

This positioning shows the outside linebacker (OLB) alignment on the tight-end (TE) side of the line. The OLB should play close to the line of scrimmage and to the TE for solid defensive coverage.

Here the OLB on the split-end (SE) side of the line has to play farther away from the line of scrimmage than the OLB on the tight-end side because the SE poses a deep or wide threat. The OLB has to be prepared to defend him.

How to Align the Defensive Secondary

The alignment for defensive backs in the secondary is positioned off the widest eligible receiver but may vary depending upon whether a man or zone cover is called. Three-man secondaries align differently than four-man secondaries, and the down and distance will affect distance off the ball no matter what your style of play. There are, however, general rules for both.

The cornerbacks (CB) in a three-deep system, in normal situations, align 6 to 8 yards off the line of scrimmage. If the alignment is taken off a tight end, the cornerback should be 2 to 3 yards wider than the tight end.

Cornerback (CB) alignment off the tight-end (TE) side of the offensive line. The CB should be 6 to 8 yards behind the LOS and 2 to 3 yards wider than the TE.

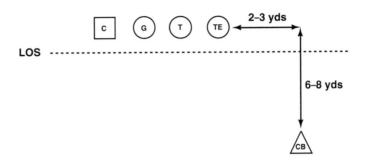

If the cornerback is defending the split-end side, he, like the outside linebacker (OLB), must recognize the threat the split end poses and must adjust accordingly. He should align head up to inside shoulder, about the same distance off the ball (see diagram below). The safety (S), as a rule of thumb, will split the two widest receivers 9 to 12 yards off the line of scrimmage (see top diagram, opposite).

The cornerback alignment off the split end (SE) is similar to that of the outside linebacker. Still 6 to 8 yards off the LOS, the cornerback will be farther away from his defensive line and prepared to cover the deep threat of the split end.

A four-deep secondary has more alignment possibilities, but a good starting point is to think of it as a half-umbrella-shaped formation. Start with the cornerbacks (CB) 4 yards off and the safeties (S) 8 to 10 yards off the line of scrimmage (see bottom diagram, opposite). The cornerbacks align just outside the tight end (TE) and the split end (SE), and the safeties align over the tight end and his ghost on the SE side.

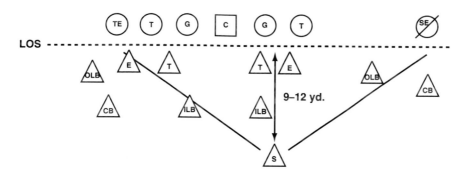

In the three-deep scenario, the safety (S) alignment should be 9 to 12 yards off the LOS and positioned between the two widest receiving threats, the TE and the SE. The safety is the last line of defense!

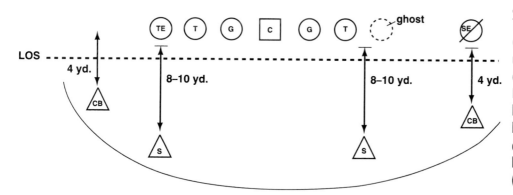

This formation is a standard and solid four-deep alignment and is good for defending against the pass. Not shown are the defensive linemen and the linebackers, but their alignment would be a seven-odd front, also known as the Oklahoma 5-2 (see pages 36–37).

The Stance for the Linemen

As a general rule of thumb, defensive linemen need to charge forward into their opposing offensive player, so their feet need a stagger in order to get good push. This is similar to a sprinter's starting position. However, too much of a stagger stance will cause a long second step, leaving the lineman vulnerable to being knocked off course. A moderate stagger of no more than one foot between heel and toe is ideal.

The critical part of the lineman's stance is hand placement. As soon as he leaves the huddle, he should find the spot that makes him as close to the line of scrimmage as possible without being offside. After he has found this spot, he can adjust to the position of the offensive lineman when he presents himself. If his hand is closest to the line of scrimmage, then his hand must be ahead of his head. This not only gives the lineman a good reference on the line of scrimmage, but it also helps him elongate the stance and put his weight forward.

The next consideration is a hands-down question: one or two. Lots of coaches have their players put both hands down to keep the charge low and prevent them from "peeking" into the backfield too soon. We prefer that the player has one hand down and the other held at a 90-degree angle poised to strike.

The last consideration is the head and eyes: they are always up and searching.

The Stance for the Linebacker

The linebacker stance is not as complicated as the stance of the defensive lineman, but it's every bit as important and demanding of precision. Remember that the linebacker has to be able to move along all the "spokes of the wheel" with almost equal quickness, so his stance needs to be balanced and athletic. Tell your linebackers to set their feet about shoulder-width apart—not too wide for the same reason of recovery we talked about with the defensive linemen. Players should stand with their knees slightly bent, back 45 degrees to the ground, and arms in front in a ready-to-hit position. The head and eyes should be up and searching.

Left: This is a good linebacker stance. Notice how he looks balanced and his *head is up*.

Right: Front view of a typical linebacker stance. Notice, however, that the feet are spread just a little too far apart; they should be no more than shoulder-width.

The Stance for the Defensive Back

The stance for a defensive back is a narrow staggered stance facing the ball. The body is low, and the weight is forward. Knees are flexed, and the back is angled slightly forward. Arms are at a 90-degree angle held forward and above the waist (see photos, opposite).

Step 2: Initial

The defense is properly positioned, the ball is snapped, and the down begins. What happens now will generally determine if your players can defend the play coming at them. The first reaction to the movement of the offense is absolutely critical to win, especially for defensive linemen. Many

line coaches, both offensive and defensive, say that "whoever gets the second foot down first will win the war."

Initial is the initial technique, by position, when the play begins. Many novice and poorly coached players will try to go directly from step 1 to step 5. They may occasionally guess right, but most of the time they'll be blocked or fouled and out of step with the play. The message for your players should be "Don't skip initial."

Initial for a Lineman

Your lineman is in his stance and ready to ignite into action. He sees both the player he's covering and the ball. Out of the corner of his eye, your lineman needs to see the ball move. The instant the ball moves, he needs to start this step in his progression. He actually has an advantage: he is moving on sight, whereas the offense is moving on sound. He needs to maximize this advantage by moving quickly.

All initial contact should be three nearly simultaneous blows struck with the shoulder and both hands. The arms should be swung like a sprinter's, close to the body with the hands open and thumbs up, and the blows should be struck with the heels of the hand. If the alignment technique is −, +, 3, 6, or 9, the inside shoulder should make contact on the offensive player's outside shoulder just under the neck, and the inside hand should go between the numbers of the offensive player. The outside hand should corral the outside arm of the offensive player, capturing the opposing player in this triangle. The lineman should keep his head at the same level as the offense, not too high, but high enough to see. As the second step of initial is underway, the lineman should create separation from the

Left: This is a typical defensive back stance for cornerbacks and safeties.

Center: A front view of the same defensive back stance.

Right: Another defensive back stance. Notice the position of the arms.

offensive player. If the technique is 0, 2, 5, 8, the lineman squares off his player's stance, and keeps his head in the gap of responsibility. Then the player creates separation. If the techniques are inside aligned, the lineman makes contact with the outside shoulder to inside shoulder, outside hand between the numbers, and corrals with the inside hand. He creates space and sheds the blocker on the second step.

Initial for a Linebacker

For the linebacker, the train of thought should be, "What can happen to me first?" Since he needs to be concerned with both run and pass coverage, he should understand that the run is the first thing that can happen and that the pass will usually be slower to develop, giving him a little longer to react. It is therefore better to prioritize the run first.

Some coaches tell the linebacker to find the spot he wants to be in and back up a little; then at the snap he should be moving forward, as he's put the run first in his thinking. He'll be a little slower to the coverage but quicker to defend the line of scrimmage from a running back. We think this is sound thinking in normal down situations. Other coaches say as long as the feet start to move, that's enough. You may agree.

For drills that work on stance alignment and initial, see Alignment Check **D1** , Stationary Mirror **D2** , and Quick Step **D3** .

Initial for the Defensive Secondary

Just as the linebacker has to prioritize threats, so do defensive backs. Because defensive backs are the last line of defense, they should begin to get leverage on the field right from the start. To facilitate this need for space, defensive backs initially back-pedal. However, some defenses that cover the deep areas with two people have the cornerbacks initially disrupt the pass routes of wide receivers. If you have a need for this tactic at your team's level of play, you'll need to understand *jamming* techniques, which are used by defensive secondary players to disrupt routes of receivers by contact (also known as *corralling*). However, for most purposes, back-pedaling will work just fine.

From the stances discussed above, the player takes a short step backward with the back foot and continues for at least three more steps, being careful to keep his weight over the knees and forward. Leaning back will cause the player to become off balance and may cause him to fall flat on his back. It's difficult enough to play in the secondary, but on the ground, on your back, it's basically impossible.

Step 3: Recognize and React

This is the essence of game preparation, providing your players with purpose and direction on the road to defending the opposition. To accomplish this you need to do your homework as a coach and create drills that best imitate your opponents' schemes so that your players recognize what the offense is going to do on any one play and where they need to be to stop it. In chapter 7, we discuss the portion of time in each practice devoted to group work. This is the time when this is best accomplished. Make up instructional cards with the schemes, routes, and blocking your opponents may throw at you. Divide your groups into teams, and while teams aren't working with the cards they can run plays. It's important that you keep your group size small and your area limited to a manageable size to maximize instruction and correction. Four at one time is a good number to accomplish both.

For this segment of teaching, split your linebackers between the defensive backs and the line. Prepare cards for line versus line and for line versus linebackers, and a separate set for backs and receivers versus defensive backs and linebackers.

It's impossible to reserve time to practice every conceivable play. As the coach, you need to decide what needs to be defended and what has to be defended, depending on the play on the field. You always have to defend the run and the pass, but with different priority levels. For example: It's third and 2. You *need* to defend the run to prevent the offense from getting the first down. Review your notes on your upcoming games and make preparations. You should think of football as a game of chess.

Step 4: Pursuit

After recognizing what the offense is trying to do and understanding the responsibilities you have taught them, your players now have the means to stop the opposition. Taking the direct route to the ball is the next step in our progression.

This is a team effort. Teach this as a team. See Pursuit **D4** .

Step 5: Tackle or Intercept

Fundamentals in athletics overlap from sport to sport, with each game having its own skill set unique to that activity. The two basic, unique fundamentals in football are blocking on the offense and tackling on the defense. Though others may need to bring an opponent to the turf, the football brand of contact is arguably the most intense. For a young player, it can be the most intimidating aspect of the sport. For those kids who are not intimidated, without proper, careful, and resolute instruction and attention to detail, it can be the most dangerous.

Form Tackling Technique

No matter how the action begins, whether a straight-on tackle from 3 yards away on a dive play or a 20-yard pursuit of a sweep back or receiver, unless your players are dragging down a player from the back, it all boils down to this technique:

Teach Safety First!

Here are some initial safeguards to incorporate in your teaching.

1. In all tackling drills, match players by size.

2. Teach technique first, and gradually add intensity of contact. This applies whether the player is a veteran or a novice.

3. In all instruction, *never* in word, thought, or deed use any language that would, in any way, lead a player to believe that using the head as a point of contact is an acceptable technique.

1. The tackler squares up on the ball carrier in a good athletic position (essentially the same position a linebacker is in at the snap).

2. The tackler aims with his eyes and keeps them focused on the target throughout the contact phase.

3. The tackler aims his shoulder at the belt buckle of the carrier, keeping his arms at a 90-degree angle, in close to his body as if curling weights, with his hands loosely cupped and his thumbs up.

#28 (left player) demonstrating initial contact on #8 for a side tackle. The tackler's head is up; again, in terms of safety, this cannot be stressed enough. Also, note how the right arm of #28 is prepared to come up and wrap around #8. Here the tackler's head is in front of the ball carrier, as it should be for a side tackle. In a straight-on tackle, the tackler's head should slide to the ball carrier's outside just prior to contact.

4. At the moment of contact, he drives his hips forward and extends his legs, causing the center of gravity of the ball carrier to go up, making him less stable. Simultaneously he brings his arm up in that curling action and grabs the jersey of the runner in the back. (Don't teach tacklers to lock their wrists around the ball carrier's back; most of the time, with all that padding, players' arms will come up short.)

5. Then he pulls the carrier tight and drives with his legs.

See Fit Position Tackling **D5** .

Intercept or "Bingo"

By rule, once the ball is in the air, both the offense and the defense have equal opportunity to catch the ball. Therefore, defensive backs need to have equally good catching and tackling skills.

Footballs are well designed for throwing, but they are difficult to catch. Just watch someone not familiar with the game try to catch one. The football needs to be caught with the fingers first and then the thumb. If the elbows are not extended, the thumbs should be on the same side of the ball, thumbs together. If the elbows need to be extended to reach the ball and an over-the-head catch is required, the thumbs need to be opposite each other. The ball then will immediately need to be "tucked" in anticipation of contact.

Whether man-to-man or zone defense, once the ball is in the air, the defensive back becomes a receiver. He needs to get out of coverage, get to the intersection point, and look for the interception. See Transition **D6** and Reaction Time **D7** .

Many Choices

This chapter on defensive football basics illustrates just some of the many possibilities for your team. Some suggested procedures are less involved, and some are much more complicated. The most important thing is to be personally confident in your own style. Certainly, you should look at other texts and remember your old high school coaches (if you played football back then). Go to a clinic at a local college or university. Most college programs have them, and many are geared to the youth game. We've never met any coach at any level who isn't free with information and isn't willing to spend the time with coaches if there's time to give.

Defensive Huddle

Have a player designated as the defensive signal caller (DSC), usually a linebacker, and place the rest of the team in position to hear his signal. Have him make an initial call to ensure that he has the team's attention. For example, the DSC might say, "Eyes!", meaning all eyes should be on him. Some DSCs say "Heads up!" to get the players' attention. During a game, the defensive huddle is used between plays in order to organize the defense and prepare for the next play.

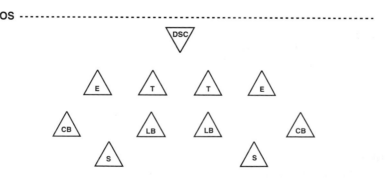

A typical defensive huddle formation. The defensive signal caller (DSC) has his back to the line of scrimmage and is facing the rest of his defensive unit to make the defensive play call.

Questions and Answers

Q. I have a few very good players. Where should the best kids play?

A. "Very good" is a vague term. In this sport, it can mean really fast, really skilled, or really aggressive. If a player is all of these, consider putting him at inside linebacker. If his lack of size is a concern, play him in the secondary.

Q. I have one kid who is very aggressive. I tried him at linebacker, but he seems to be easily fouled by the offense. What do you suggest?

A. First, examine your coaching methods with him. If he's truly aggressive, you want very much for him to succeed at linebacker. If you've adjusted your approach, and he still has discipline trouble, try making him a defensive end. Looking ahead, most college coaches recruit only these kinds of kids and then do just what you're doing. The ones who can play linebacker play linebacker. The ones who can't become defensive ends.

Q. You suggested discipline trouble above, but that's not the problem. This is a great kid, and he tries very hard.

A. Remember, athletic discipline has to do with self-control and may have nothing at all to do with bad behavior. Discipline in this sense is doing what the coach tells you to do even when your instincts tell you to do something else. If you're instructing him properly, and if he, even with great effort, is always in the wrong spot, he's not a disciplined athlete. Putting him at defensive end will give him a little less to think about.

Q. I have one defensive lineman who is among the league's best, whereas my others are average players. This player has been playing left tackle, but it seems that the teams we play run away from him. How can I get him more involved?

A. There are two immediate issues to consider. Watch the opponents and look for tendencies. You were smart to put your best defensive lineman on the left, as most offensive teams run to the right. However, your opponents are doing something different. It may be that they are running away from your star, but you can make some adjustments, too. If you see that they like to run to a tight-end side, have your player always go to that side. He may have to make a technique adjustment, but you're a good coach and can help him with that. You may also want to consider an "odd" defensive set and put your player nose to nose with their center.

Q. What exactly is the "blitz"?

A. Blitzes can be different things to different coaches. Generally they are schemes where linebackers or defensive backs are committed to a pass rush. Most of the time, man-to-man coverage is played behind them. So instead of having only four players rushing, you can, through blitzing, have five, six, seven, or even eight players after the passer.

Q. I have a player who's very timid. I would like to talk to his parents, but I don't know how to approach them because his dad is really enthusiastic.

A. If this player is trying and seems to like being a part of the group, then you should not give up on him, but keep him in drills that aren't over his head. Keep encouraging him, and if you see some progress, then give him new challenges. If you don't, don't push him and don't be too critical. He knows he's having a problem, and so do the other kids. It's youth ball, so let him progress slower if he needs to.

If he can't protect himself, you have to face the situation and talk to the parents. It will be worse if the player gets hurt, both physically and mentally.

Q. I have three players who are very aggressive and intimidate the rest of the team. If I split them up, the kids they drill with only learn how to get back up. If I put them together, they'll beat up on each other.

A. Initially they need to be grouped together. Simply use a quick whistle when the hitting becomes too intense, and be thankful you have them. Use them as demonstrators so the others can see what you like about them. Eventually one of the others will break away from the crowd to become your fourth. Hopefully this will begin a progression of youngsters who catch on.

Q. I have a parent who says he doesn't want his child to play defense, because he'll get hurt. What should I say?

A. Well, the short answer is that you're the coach, this is a team game, and the player needs to be placed where he can best help the team, in the coach's opinion. He might not even be a player you want on the defense. Then tell the parent not to worry about the differences between offensive and defensive positions in this age group.

CHAPTER 5

Essential Skills: Offensive Football

This chapter goes over the fundamentals of offensive football. For many players, offense is where it's at. Breakaway runs and long passes are what the cameras follow on TV. Rightfully so—they are exciting and powerful images of the sport and attract people to the game. Those who are more than casual observers of the sport, however, know that the essence of offensive football is in the melding of eleven different job responsibilities and rule restrictions into a single-minded unit. From basic formations, to running with the ball, to passing, to kicking, to proper blocking techniques and more, you'll be introduced to the skills your players need to create a cohesive offense. This information, combined with the drills in chapter 11, will help you get started and get your offense working toward scoring their first points.

The Mission

The object of the offense is to score. In order to score touchdowns the ball needs to cross over the goal line while in possession of the offense. The two ways this can occur is if an offensive player runs over the goal line with the ball or if an offensive player catches a forward pass in the end zone. As an offensive coach, you have the responsibility of developing strategies that will help your team accomplish this primary objective. In developing your offensive philosophy, you need to balance two conflicting dynamics: to have enough offensive strategies to attack the opposition effectively and to keep the strategies simple enough so that all the players can master their assignments.

A third concern (maybe more important than the first two) is matching what you would like to do with what your players are capable of doing. Remember, the kids will try to do anything you ask them to do; it's your job to make sure they *can* do what you ask.

Attacking the Defense with the Running Game

In developing the running game, there are some things that you should keep in mind about defensive football before you begin. Remember, the defense is set up, at least initially, to defend the whole field, so the forces trying to stop you are spread out. The offense, however, will be concentrating on puncturing one spot in the defense and breaking through before the defense recognizes the point of attack and sends reinforcements. Timing and quickness are essential.

There are two basic methods to accomplish this task in the running game: the power running game and the finesse running game. *Power running* involves overwhelming a gap with players and knocking the defenders off, or away from, the ball and the ball carrier. The power game is easy to teach as the blocking is straightforward, and the backfield action is usually not very complex. In using this method expect short gains and short quarters as a rule.

Finesse running has two separate trains of thought. One theory is to isolate a defender on two potential ball carriers and see which player he covers. If he defends player A, then player B will carry the ball; if he defends player B, then player A carries. This is known as the *option*. The quarterback moves along the line of scrimmage, and a predetermined defensive player is left unblocked. A diving or trailing back is the quarterback's option. When mastered, this is extremely effective football. Mastering it, however, is a highly time-consuming process and is dependent on one player's decision making and on your ability to instill in him the skills to make those decisions. You're also exposing your quarterback to an unblocked lineman and the risk of injury, which is one reason why many youth coaches avoid the option play or use it selectively.

The second type of finesse running game involves widening the gaps in the defense by angle blocking and delaying the pursuit of the defense with some decoy or misdirection action in the backfield. This is not as difficult to teach as the option, but there is much more for you and your players to learn than in the power game. The importance of this thinking is that it's less demanding physically, and if your team is physically overmatched, it gives them a means of fooling the defense rather than trying to "beat them up." Additionally, it spreads the responsibility more evenly throughout the offensive unit.

Running the Clock

Incomplete passes stop the game clock. Running plays result in fewer game stoppages and, consequently, shorter or "faster" quarters, since the clock keeps ticking. If your kids are bigger and stronger than their opponents, this can be very effective. If this is the only part of your running game, be prepared to see additional defenders near the line of scrimmage, as well.

You need to assess your own abilities, knowledge, and the relative strength of your players in formulating an offensive playbook. Most coaches include a little of each—finesse and power—even though they may rely on one more than the other.

Attacking the Defense with the Passing Game

The passing game can be subdivided into four different schemes: drop-back passing, sprint-out passing, quick passing, and play-action passes. As with the running game, it's good to have a little of each in your playbook even though you may favor one over the other.

Drop-back passing is probably the kind of passing most associated with the air attack in football. The quarterback drops straight back from the center in the middle of the offensive formation, sets up, throws the ball downfield or toward the side line, or swings the ball to the flanks. He usually takes five steps to set up, but in some schemes it's a seven-step drop. This allows for a balanced passing attack right or left. It's pretty standard stuff, but it can be tough if your quarterback is short or does not have a particularly strong arm.

Sprint-out passing is a passing style where the quarterback attacks a flank after receiving the snap, instead of going straight back. This gives him a choice of running or throwing. This can be effective with a shorter quarterback or one with a weaker arm because it makes the pass a shorter delivery. Lots of coaches hang their hats on the sprint-out game, but it's limited because it favors the sprint side and makes passes to the other side very problematic. If your quarterback is not a thrower, and you want to have a minimal passing game, this may be your only option.

Quick passing involves a quick delivery after a two- or three-step drop. The pass needs to go only 5 to 8 yards downfield to a slanting or quick-releasing receiver and is effective against defensive backs that are too deep or linebackers who are too close. Offensive linemen will need to incorporate techniques to keep defensive linemen's hands down.

Play-action passes are designed to complement running plays and use the same backfield action as running plays. The quarterback withdraws the ball after faking the handoff. He then either continues in the same direction, looking for a receiver, or moves against the flow to find a target. These are effective plays, especially if you've been a good running team and your play-action passes come off your best running plays. They're much less effective in long-yardage situations because the time spent in the play action keeps your quarterback from focusing on the receivers. In these situations, the defense largely ignores the running action because they know you need to pass to keep the ball.

The same rules apply in selecting how you want to use the passing game. Look over your personnel and assess their strengths and weaknesses.

Evaluate your opponents and choose your weapons. There's a tendency to discount the passing game at younger levels, but you need to have some sort of passing game in your plans. If you don't, you'll see many more defenders in position to stop your running game.

Formations of Attack

Formations are not philosophies, but they do tell you what you can do or will have trouble doing. In other words, some formations are better at doing some things than others. After you've decided your means of moving the football, you need to put your squad in a formation that best allows them to accomplish the task at hand. In doing this, be careful not to tip off the opposition to your intent by being in a predictable formation. Remember: Don't give the opposing coach any more opportunities to beat you.

The Offense Is Always Outmanned

After the quarterback hands off the ball or passes it, he generally becomes a nonplayer, which makes the player ratio 11:10. You have to have someone carrying the ball on running plays, bringing the ratio to 11:9. When you throw the ball downfield, it's going into enemy territory. No matter how hard they try, offensive linemen are hard-pressed to be a factor downfield (11 on fewer than 9).

The Line

By rule you need to have seven players on the line of scrimmage. You can have more, but you must have at least seven. So what are the possibilities here? Well, you can play with a line with two tight ends (TE) as shown in the diagram. This is a strong running set, and for the dive and off-tackle running game you can't beat it. It balances your threats left and right, and keeps the defense off balance. For perimeter plays, however, you'll need additional help from a flanking back to help secure the corner. If you want your ends to be receivers, their releases to get free and open are subject to interference from the defensive front as well.

The offensive line set up for a strong running game with the two tight ends (TE) in position to block any threats coming from the left or right side.

Alternatively, you can have an offensive line with two split ends (SE). This is a good passing formation because your ends, who are the quick-receiving threats, are split away from the front and are less likely to be held up. However, you need to have an effective passing game for this formation,

The effectiveness of this passing formation with two split ends (SE) will depend on the age of your kids and their throwing ability. If you don't have a passing threat, stick to using the two tight-end formation; otherwise the defense will ignore the intended threat of the two split ends and concentrate on defending against your running game.

or you'll have no running game. Without the threat of a pass, the defense will ignore the split ends and defend the run for which you now have two fewer blockers.

The compromise is, of course, one split end and one tight end. The tight-end/split-end line set is the industry standard, so to speak. Everyone uses it. There's no rule about how many players should be on each side of the ball, and many coaches make their lines unbalanced by putting both guards or tackles or ends on the same side of the ball. Called *overformations*, they can be a problem for defenses to recognize and practice for.

The compromise offensive set, one tight end (TE) and one split end (SE), uses the best of both formations.

The *overformation* is simply making your line unbalanced on either side of the center. In the first example, both guards are side by side on the same side of the center. Other variations include placing both tackles (T) on the same side and next to each other, or your tight end (TE) and split end (SE) off to the same side; of course, the split end would be a few yards away from the TE. These types of formations can confuse a defense.

The Backs

Let's assume that our discussion is confined to variations of formations where the quarterback is taking a hand-to-hand snap from the center. There are no rules for the positioning of backs, except that in order to remain backs, they must be off the line of scrimmage. So the positioning of backs is generally a coach's decision to get the best people in the best location to make the play work. The choices are numerous, but below are a few popular backfield sets to consider in formulating your offensive package.

Let's use all three backs in the backfield as a starting point. This set is called the *Straight T* or *Full House* alignment. If you've decided on the power game, this set is for you, especially if your fullback (FB) is your strongest inside runner. Halfbacks (HB) for lead blockers make this a formidable inside attacking formation. If your strongest inside runner is a halfback, you may consider putting him behind the fullback. This gives you an extremely strong side for the offensive attack. This is the *Power I*. While both of these formations are strong inside running attacks, both the Power I and the Straight T are weak at the flank, unless you're going to option. Neither of these sets is a passing threat formation.

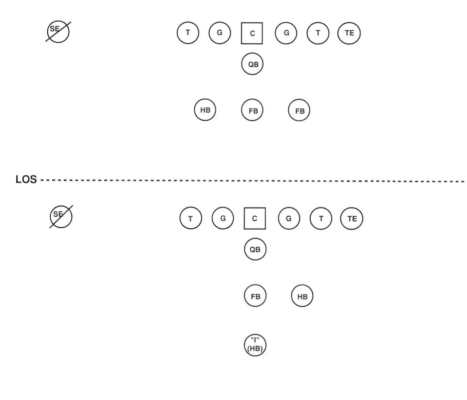

The Straight T or Full House utilizes all three backs in the backfield. This is a great set for the power running game. If your fullback (FB) is a strong runner, the two halfbacks (HB) make great lead blockers for an inside (up the middle) running game.

The Power I utilizes a strong running halfback ("I"). With that player lined up behind the fullback (FB) you have a good strong-side running formation with both the FB and the other halfback ready to lead block. In this diagram, the right side is the strong side and would likely be the side that your runners attack.

There is an adjustment that can be made to both sets to help seal a corner and establish the beginnings of a perimeter assault. You can move the remaining halfback to a flanking position on the tight-end or split-end side. This creates a *wing* or *slot formation* (see diagrams next page). In order to secure both flanks, you can place backs in the wing position on both sides of the formation.

A wing alignment with one of the halfbacks (HB) moving up to the tight-end (TE) side of the formation and becoming a wing back (W).

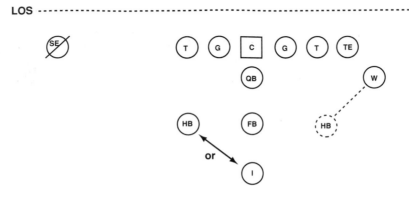

A slot alignment showing the one of the halfbacks (HB) becoming the slot back (SB).

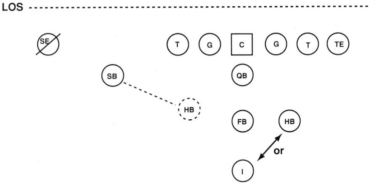

A double-wing formation utilizes both halfbacks (HB) as wing backs (W). This helps protect the flanks of the formation.

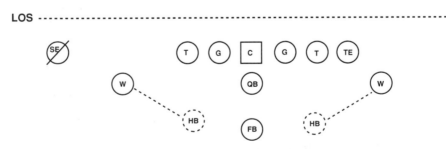

If you would like to widen your offensive set to either spread the defense or facilitate the passing game, you could use one of your backfield positions for a receiving player by flanking him like a split end. This is the classic pro formation (see top diagram, opposite).

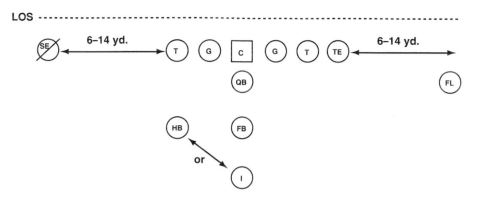

The classic pro formation is designed to spread the defense and help open up the passing game by positioning one of your backfield players as a receiver out to the side like a split end, but known as a flanker (FL).

The previous examples show a fullback in line with the ball, but many coaches use a "split" backfield with the fullback set to the tight-end side.

LOS --

Many coaches offset the fullback (FB) to the tight-end (TE) side of the formation. This is known as a *split backfield* or *split backs*.

A Word about Motion

On the offense, you can put a back in motion and keep him moving as the ball is snapped. This can allow you to show one formation out of the huddle and change it just before the snap. Motion is legal if only one player has moved, if he started to move after the team has stopped for one second as a unit, and if he is not moving toward the line of scrimmage at the snap.

Simplicity

The possibilities of mixing and matching the line and backfield sets are almost endless. Remember, though, you won't need—nor should you attempt—to include all of them in your playbook. Balance your needs with what your kids can absorb. If you err, do so on the side of simplicity.

Final Thoughts on Offensive Thinking

In formulating your plans of attack, focus on attacking the entire front. Have a sweep attack and an off-tackle attack and an inside game. In thinking about your passing game, first determine the skills of your quarterback and receivers before you finalize any plans. This will be a great discussion at your coaches' meeting.

Teaching Offensive Skills and Drills

Offensive skills are more specific and defined than defensive skills. Because position responsibility is so different from group to group, separation for teaching fundamental skills is essential.

Unless they're in motion, each offensive player must begin in an offensive stance. As with the defense, stances can be different depending on what position you play.

Stance for Linemen

Coaches who want their linemen to fire straight ahead or only at slight angles left or right will also want their linemen to have the bulk of their weight forward. They also may choose to have one hand down in a three-point stance or put both hands down in a four-point stance. The feet are staggered about toe to heel and slightly wider than the shoulders. The head is held up with the neck "bulled."

Left: A balanced three-point stance, as seen here, can be used by all offensive positions (except the quarterback!).

Right: The front view of the same three-point stance. The head is up!

Coaches who expect the linemen to be able to move equally in all directions will coach their players to assume a more balanced stance. In a three-point stance, the points form a scalene triangle (in which the sides are of unequal length), with the player's weight only slightly on his hand or hands. (When a player knows his assignment is straight ahead, he can hide more weight on his hand.) The feet are only slightly staggered, with toe to instep. Because players may be moving sideways as well as forward, they should narrow their stance so their feet are just shoulder width apart and pointing straight ahead, or with their heels slightly out. To work on proper stance, see Bird Dog **01** .

Stance for Backs

If you want the backs in a three-point stance, they would use the same stance as the one for linemen, except that the tail is down slightly. Instead, you may want your backs in a two-point stance, a balanced stance with the weight only slightly over the toes, every joint slightly flexed, and the hands resting on the tops of the thigh pads. False steps are a common problem but not a great concern. If your back false steps a lot, move him closer to where you want him to go.

Left: This is a nicely balanced two-point running back stance.

Right: A side view of the two-point offensive back stance.

Blocking

Just as tackling is the unique skill of the defense, blocking is its counterpart on the offense. It's not found in the same form in any other sport. Blocking, however, is not always the same, as positions require different skills. Blocking is executed in a variety of techniques depending on who is blocking and who is being blocked.

Drive Blocking

The purpose of the drive block is to push the defender off the line of scrimmage. After exploding out of his stance, the blocker makes contact with his shoulder and then with his hands (see photo next page). At the instant of contact, the blocker drives his hips forward to raise the center of gravity of the defender and create backward momentum. Once this momentum is delivered, the player can turn the defender in the direction he wants the defender to go.

A player demonstrating a lead block (in this case a drive block) on #11 for ball carrier #4 (left).

Angle Blocking

The purpose of the angle block is to block down on a defender in the blocker's inside gap or on the head of a defender inside. The blocking action begins with a very short directional step with the inside foot into the neutral zone. It needs to be short so that the next step won't be long. The blocker's primary contact should be with his outside shoulder to prevent penetration and keep the inside gap open. The inside hand should be placed between the numbers and the outside hand on the side of the defensive lineman. Again, as momentum is delivered, your player turns the defender and works his hips into the hole to prevent penetration.

Reach Blocking

The purpose of the reach block is to open an outside gap, the idea being to "hook" a defender who is on your blocker's head or already outside him. The block uses a directional step like the angle block, but it's to the outside. The blocker must get his inside shoulder outside the defender as quickly as possible and after contact work hard to wheel his hips to an outside position.

Pass Blocking

The technique of pass blocking is for drop-back protection. When designing your schemes for blocking for the pass, the rule is "big on big." What this means is to design your blocking so that offensive linemen block defensive linemen. The skill is to get set quickly and step with the inside foot first to prevent penetration inside. It's your preference whether to force contact by having players step forward to stop the initial defensive charge, or to brace for it by stepping back. Whichever you decide on, the next phase is to let the defender create the pressure and to have your blocker control it. The blocker should extend his arms, prevent quick access to the passer, and then steer the defender away. Like a good wrestler, the blocker should let the pressure of the defensive lineman or linebacker work against him. See Blocking Squares **02** and Onion **03** .

Pulling Linemen

Pulling linemen move behind adjacent teammates to beef up the blocking. The purpose of pulling linemen is to get more manpower at the point of attack, especially at the flanks, or to create a trapping situation by allowing defenders to penetrate the line of scrimmage and then block them at an angle with linemen running laterally in back of the line of scrimmage. The blocks described below can apply to a pulling lineman as well; this lineman is just moving to a new spot to do them. Two easy drills to assist you in teaching both these techniques are Pull and Trap **04** and Pull and Lead **05** .

Downfield Blocking

In blocking away from the line of scrimmage, aggressive contact might get you into foul trouble. A good coaching strategy is to tell your player to mirror intensity. If the defender is coming hard, your player should hit hard. If the defender is playing soft, your player can play "soft ball." In this case, we coach "hit them high and don't hurt them." Your player should maintain contact and let the ball carrier choose the route.

Moving the Ball on the Ground

Offensive backs carry the ball in the running game and are used as receivers in the passing game. Wide-outs and tight ends are receivers who occasionally may be involved in the running game. Their duties as contributors to the cause mean that they must carry out every assignment: faking runs and routes or, more importantly, blocking with as much resolve as they show when "fighting for every yard." Good backs and ends do it all.

The "Eligibles" in the Running Game

As we look at the skills necessary to be a good running back or receiver, let's again work from the moment of contact and backpedal to the skills after stance. Remember that, at some point in the play, the passing game turns into the running game. Coaches like to talk about YAC, yards after catch. Therefore, in this vein, every eligible receiver is a runner.

"Be a Hitter: Never Stop Your Feet"

The best running backs hit before they are hit. Walter Payton, the great Chicago Bears runner, was the master of delivering a blow to the tackler. The technique is for the player to gather himself in a low position as contact becomes imminent, showing the defender shoulder pads and knees. Then the back delivers a forearm blow with his free hand as he leads in and initiates contact. This will partially neutralize the defensive player's momentum and allow your player to get extra distance on his run.

Keeping the feet moving throughout the contact phase is not only good football running, but a great safety skill as well. Leg injuries generally happen when the foot is planted, but moving feet are tough targets. See Big Hitter **06** .

Warding Off

Contact may be fun, but if the running back can avoid it, he'll have a better chance of scoring. A back can prevent contact by using his hand on the defender to ward him off. The best spot to do this is at the helmet. Here, timing is critical. As the defender bows his head to launch toward the runner's hip, the runner pushes the defender's head down with a stiff arm. See Stiff Arm **07** .

"Cause Him to Miss"

Good backs develop the skills of faking. If the back can cause the defender to lose his leverage on his position, the back may fool the defender altogether, with no need to knock him back or stiff-arm him. The key is to get the defender's weight to move in one direction and be centered over one leg. Once his weight is on one leg and the other is in the air, the back can easily get around the defender by running in the opposite direction. See Escape **08** .

Carrying a Football

The grip on the ball can change with the relative position of the carrier to the line of scrimmage and possible threats to keeping control of the ball. The question here is safety or speed. If safety is a big concern—that is, safely maintaining possession—you could teach your ball carriers to cover the ball with both hands. This is accomplished by the player grabbing both points of the ball and rolling his chest over it. The ball is safe, but the player runs slower with no arms to swing. Frankly, most of the time this is unnecessary. Both speed and safety can be accomplished by adjusting the one-hand carry. The best way to teach this is for players to learn the passer's grip and then tuck the ball between the upper arm and the chest. Players can adjust for speed by swinging their arms to create speed in the open and then can squeeze hard when control is a concern. Don't have your players squeeze the ball and swing their arms at the same time because the resulting action will cause the ball to "squirt out" and result in a fumble.

Left: A good running position for the ball carrier.

Right: And a good ball grip.

Getting the Ball

Getting the ball means two things: the handoff and the catch. There is no other way to get the ball, except to recover a fumble, and it's best not to try to run after a fumble recovery. The fingers are extended as far as possible, the catch is made in the fingers, and the thumbs grip just after the catch is made. The ball is immediately tucked away as described above, and the catcher becomes a runner.

What is new here is the concept of routes or pass patterns. Coaches teach routes from a *passing tree*, so called because each pattern comes off the release or the trunk of the tree. The release is the first step a receiver uses to get off the line of scrimmage. It varies from back to wide-out to tight end. From this the routes are numbered depending on the play-calling system chosen by the coach.

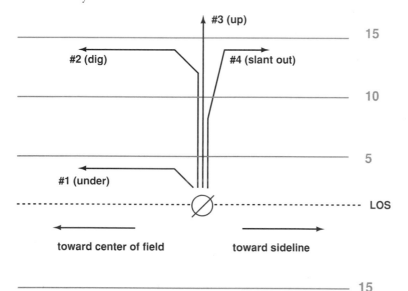

This passing tree illustrates different passing routes (also known as pass patterns) and their associated numbers. Any numbers can be assigned, but keep it simple for your quarterback and your receivers!

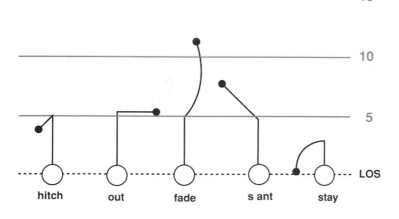

Here are some more common routes that receivers run. All breaks from the initial direction are typically at 5 yards, with the exception of the stay route, in which the receiver turns around after just a few yards and comes back to catch a short pass.

The Handoff

The hand-to-hand exchange between the quarterback and the ball carrier is a straightforward technique, and once you establish responsibilities, it can be easily mastered. Depending on your personal philosophy, the quarterback presents the ball to the carrier with either a one- or two-handed pass. The carrier passes the quarterback with his inside elbow up, forming the top boundary of a target pocket for the quarterback. The arm should be held lower than the shoulder and not too wide, to prevent the carrier's elbow from hitting on the quarterback's helmet. His outside arm forms the base of the target. His hand is at the bottom of the belly, palm up. As the carrier feels the ball enter the pocket, he closes over it and assumes a grip on the ball. It's important that the ball carrier trusts the quarterback to place the ball in the pocket. He must concentrate on seeing the openings in the line, rather than looking for the ball. See Quick Look **09** , Focus **010** , Hand Off and Hit **011** , Centers and Quarterbacks **012** , Skeleton **013** , and Half Line **014** .

Left: A good demonstration of handoff technique. Notice the arm position of #11.

Right: Handoff technique continued. #11 (left) has inside elbow up to quarterback (right) allowing for easy delivery of the ball.

The Quarterback

The quarterback's skills need special attention. We've already put him into position with the ball after the exchange with the center, and we've discussed handoff technique. What makes the position of quarterback special and the player in the position special is the impact that an effective passing game can have on the success of a team.

Depending on the age of your quarterback and your team, the passing game will either be a minor part of your offense or a major part. Start slowly and assess the individual skills of your quarterback *and* your receivers. If the ability is not there, stick to a running game! Don't put unnecessary pressure on your quarterback to attempt a passing game.

When you look at the game from Paul Brown (the inventor of the modern-day passing game) and Otto Graham (Paul Brown's quarterback with the Cleveland Browns in the 1940s and 1950s) to Bill Belichek (the coach of the New England Patriots) and Tom Brady (the Patriots' quarterback), the coach-quarterback relationship has proven the most important to a team's success. Develop a positive relationship with the player who leads your team. If your team is to develop confidence around this player, you have to show confidence and patience with him. This doesn't mean treating him differently, but you'll need to treat him as "special," for on many occasions the focus and pressure will be more on him than others on your team.

Passing the Football

No matter what style you choose to use for your passing game, the thrower must have certain fundamentals that are characteristic of all throwing techniques. The passer should grip the ball primarily with the middle finger and thumb. He should position his hand so that the fingers are over the laces—except for the index finger, which is positioned toward the end of the ball. The passer grips the ball away from the palm as much as possible and cocks his wrist.

At the beginning of the throwing action, the ball should be held in both hands near ear level. As the throwing action begins, the ball is higher than the elbow, and the elbow is higher than the shoulder. The shoulder is closed near the chin as the ball is held, but it's snapped open as the throwing action begins. The hips are closed with the shoulders and snap open slightly ahead of the shoulders. The throwing stance is light and bouncy. The stride is normally short, and the weight is transferred to a slightly turned in front foot. In the follow-through, the hand rotates forward and then down, so that the index finger is a guide to the direction of the ball, and the thumb is pointing at the ground. The hips cross the perpendicular line with the flight of the ball, and the trailing leg meets the other or leaves the ground. See One-Knee Passing **015** and Fast Drop **016** .

Left: The standard passing grip. Notice the position of the quarterback's right hand on the football's laces.

Center: An example of poor passing technique: the throwing elbow is down, the ball is held too low, and the hips are closed.

Right: An example of good passing technique: the elbow is higher than the shoulder, and the hips are open.

Questions and Answers

Q. I've seen two of the teams we'll play. It seems to me one plays man-to-man defense and the other plays a zone defense. How do I attack them?

A. In attacking man-to-man defenses, run some crossing patterns with your receivers in passing and attack the perimeter on running plays. Zone teams will generally see the ball better, so use short passes and try to have your receivers run in between defenders.

Q. My best runner is also my best thrower. Where should I play him?

A. What do the rest of your passers look like? If they are good receivers, you may want to put this player at quarterback and build your offense around a multithreat position. If you don't have a couple of players like him, be careful, because you don't want to build your plans around a position that won't exist if he gets hurt. Another thought is to design some plays with the halfback option (HBO). In that position this player can attack the flank, run or throw, and use his skills from the halfback spot.

Q. I have a player who has trouble staying on his feet when he makes a cut. What can I do to help him?

A. Have this player work on planting his outside foot before he cuts. This usually helps from a technique standpoint. Also, check to make sure his shoes fit properly.

CHAPTER 6

Essential Skills: The Kicking Game

If, in fact, the kicking game is the third phase of the game of football, then first-string players should be included. The major requirement for these teams is just sheer effort. The biggest plays with the most yards to be gained or lost are in this aspect of the sport. If you are thinking of a place for special awards, give them here. Teams often give out special recognition awards. For example, Ohio State University coaches give out Buckeye stickers for each big play a player makes, and these stickers are showcased on player helmets. You might consider similar awards. This chapter will cover the fundamentals of the kicking game, both the kickoff and punting. In conjunction with the drills in chapter 12, you'll have the foundation to the all-important kicking game.

The Defensive Kicking Game

The Kickoff

Hopefully your team does a lot of kickoffs, since they're done every time your team scores. The first type of kickoff is the *lane cover*. This is the simplest, and therefore easiest, to teach. The ball is kicked from between the hash marks, at the 35-yard line in college, or the 40-yard line in high school, Pop Warner, and youth leagues. (However, some youth leagues require that instead of a kickoff on the change of possesion, or at the start of the game or half, the ball be placed on the offense's own 35-yard line. This is usually done with younger players.) The ten cover players stay in equally divided lanes until they converge on the ball (see left diagram next page). See Lane Coverage **K1** .

You may choose to send down staggered walls of defenders, instead of the lane coverage (see right diagram next page). This involves three waves of players attacking with different techniques at different times. The advantage of this is that it discourages man-to-man assignment blocking. The first

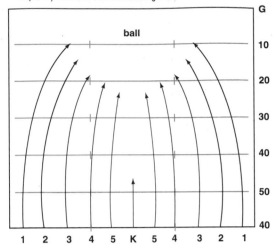

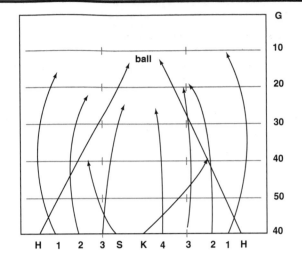

Left: Lane coverage is critical during the kickoff. This diagram shows the field divided equally into tenths and the lanes the players cover. Your kicker (K) should stay back as a safety just in case the runner makes it through the defense.

Right: A three-wave kickoff formation utilizes two "hot men" (H) as a first wave. They should follow and go directly to the ball. The next wave consists of seven players (1, 2, 3, 4, 3, 2, 1) who stay in their assigned lanes. Two safeties (a safety and your kicker) stay back as the last line of defense, or third wave, against the return run.

wave is called *hot men* or *bullets*. Their job is to go right to the ball. They have no lane responsibility and can just "play tough." Specifically, they want the ball carrier to have to alter his route or be delayed. The second wave is made up of seven players who have lane responsibility; like the first coverage, the lane adjusts with the relative position of the ball left or right. The third wave consists of two safeties (one safety and the kicker) who stay back just in case the return runner gets through the first two waves. They are your last line of defense.

The Punt

It's fourth down, and technically you're still on offense, but if you're going to punt the ball away, you had better prepare to play defense. What formation you choose to punt from is wholly dependent on one player: your long snapper or center. This is definitely a position to hold tryouts for (see sidebar). If your punter is good, you can get better coverage downfield. The shorter the distance from snapper to punter, the more blockers you have to keep for protection, the fewer players can go downfield quickly to cover the return, and the greater the chance for your opponents to gain significant yardage. The blocking rule here is to block until you hear the thud of the ball being kicked.

How To Find and Select a Long Snapper

While your center generally snaps the ball to your quarterback, your long snapper is not necessarily the same player. This is a good position to hold tryouts for. Have the players trying out perform the following procedure. Your goal is to find a player who can consistently snap the ball 10 to 15 yards.

The snapper starts by making a stationary forward pass. The snapper then makes the same forward pass with the other hand on the ball as well, but using the fingers on that hand only for stability and guidance. Repeat the previous step until the snapper can make a 10- to 15-yard pass using this technique. Then, the snapper bends over and makes the same pass through his legs.

If you have a player on your team who can make this pass, you've found your long snapper.

How to Find and Select a Punter

Like selecting a snapper, finding a punter may require tryouts. You never know what you'll discover. Here are the basics of punting a football.

The punter cradles the ball with slightly bent arms extended at waist level and then drops so that the ball is parallel with the ground. Then the punter takes two steps, beginning with his kicking foot. On the third step the punter swings his leg through and strikes the ball with his foot pointed and ankle flexed. If struck well, the ball will spiral. Keep in mind that the distance of your players' punts and the success of your punting game depend on the ages of your players. See Perfect Contact **K2** .

The progression of responsibility begins with the inside gap, to any player straight ahead, to the player on the outside gap. The lane principle applies.

The Tight Punt Formation

A tight punt formation indicates that the line splits (spacing) are reduced. Typically this is used when kicking from your own goal line, meaning that there is not room for the standard 15 yards between the line and the kicker.

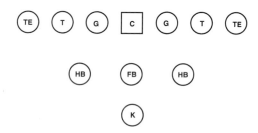

The standard tight punt formation. Notice how all of the players are closely grouped together.

The Spread Punt Formation

The spread punt (the line is spread across the field) is better for return coverage, and is used when a long snap ensures that the defenders won't have enough time to rush in and block the kick provided their paths are even minimally disrupted. Therefore, the rule here is to make your players disrupt the defenders, restart, run downfield, and go cover the return. Because it's a quick cover, either lane or wave rush is fine. In both philosophies, the players covering the ends want to narrow the field.

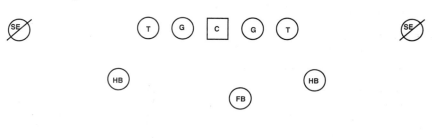

The spread punt formation is the opposite of the tight punt. The spacing between players has increased dramatically. Typically, this formation is better for covering the return run.

Field Goal Blocks

If you have a need to block a field goal, use your short-yardage or goal line defense and be creative. Remember your opponent is coaching players not to let anyone inside, so the fastest route will probably be from the flanks. You might want to send someone at the outside shoulder of the widest offensive player and try to sneak someone underneath.

The Offensive Kicking Game

Kickoff Return

Left: A wall return from a 5-2-1-2-1 alignment. Five players are up front: the two tackles (T), the two guards (G), and the center (C). The two players behind them are the ends (E). Then you have one fullback (FB), two backs (B), and, most importantly, the ball carrier (BC). Note that the downfield players retreat to blocking positions as soon as the kicked ball is past them.

In returning the kickoff you'll need to initially defend the field 50 yards deep. Since the kickoff is a free kick, after the ball has traveled 10 yards it's a free ball and either team can recover it. Spreading the field is necessary to ensure possession. Five blockers are generally kept near the restraining line, 10 yards from the ball. Where everyone else goes is a matter of personal coaching decisions. Some like a 2-2-2 funnel arrangement; some like a 2-1-2-1 setup or variations on both.

There are a number of philosophies regarding the best way to get the most yards from the kick return. You may choose to make a frontal assault with a *wall return*, where you set a wedge-type blocking maneuver and have your return player look for a seam to run through. You might, however, try a *sweep return*, a sweeping end run with your blockers forming a lane by walling off the kickoff team.

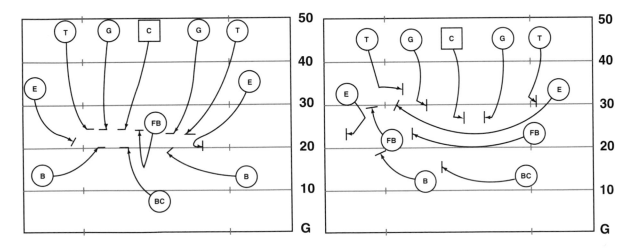

Right: A sweep return from a 5-2-2-2 alignment.

Points after Touchdowns and Field Goals

The tight punt alignment is also a possibility for the place-kicking downs. Just replace a blocker with the holder and move him to 7 yards off the ball. The inside gap needs to be secured with no leakage. Remember that field goals are scrimmage downs; as with a punt, your team has to cover any kick not going into the end zone.

Place Kicker

With all the soccer taught in youth programs and all the attention given to the position of place kicker, you should have many prospects for the kicking position. What a place kicker needs to develop is a rhythm that promotes consistency. Remember: A kickoff is used to start a game or after a score is made. The place kick is used for an attempted point after a touchdown or field goal. The ball holder stands 6.5 yards behind the center. Although 6- to 12-year-olds rarely kick a successful field goal, it doesn't hurt to teach them the fundamentals.

CHAPTER 7

The Practice

Running a football practice as the head coach is a lot like being a school principal. The day begins with attendance. Then the students go to their individual classes for instruction in one phase of the curriculum. The bell rings, and they are off to second period for a different experience, maybe with the same students or maybe with new ones. They go from period to period with instruction all along the way. Then at the end of the day they have an assembly where they all work together, listen to some important announcements, and go home. If there's a textbook involved, you may assign homework.

Well, here you're the principal, and your assistants are the teachers. The test is the game on the weekend. If you win the game, you pass. If you are less successful, you review what you taught and how you taught it, and work harder next time for the new test. Unlike school, however, the parents not only are present to watch you give the test but may also have been at your lessons, too. That's one of the positives in athletics: kids and their parents involved in a great activity.

Be Consistent

Start on time. If you say your practice begins at 6:00 P.M., it begins at 6:00 P.M. Stay on time. If you say it will be a 2-hour practice, stay within that time frame as closely as you can. This helps to establish discipline in your players and will be appreciated by their parents. Occasions will come along when your guys are on a roll, things are going well, and you want to squeeze in one more play or two. This is a good time to stay an extra 5 minutes, but don't push it. If things are going well, then your team has worked hard for you, and fatigue may become an injury concern. If things are not going well, you're not going to gain anything late in practice that was missing all night long. Find a positive way to end the workout and encourage better work for the next time. Never beat a dead horse or a spent athlete.

Follow a Routine

Try to make your practices build on a routine. You can waste a lot of time when kids are standing around wondering where to go next. If your practice is a routine or a progression, players will get to know what's coming next and won't have to be directed to a location or to a particular coach. Warm up the same way, stretch the same way, do your fundamental period at the same relative place in your practice schedule. A sequence of group work, mixed group work, kicking game work, and team time makes practice time more efficient.

Have a Plan

Between the two of us, we've spent nearly sixty years doing what you're about to begin. Neither one of us would ever step onto a practice field and coach by the seat of our pants. Each practice is planned so that nearly every second is directed toward the teaching and preparation of our teams. You and your assistants should have a good idea what will be happening at each juncture of the practice session. Make out a practice plan for each workout. Be precise on time amounts and personnel involved. Assign groups to coaches and to skill areas to work on. If you're going to have groups work together, have it down on your plan. If you're going to mix groups, such as having the defensive line work with the linebacker, have a designated period of time for this to happen in your plan.

Give Your Assistants Responsibility

At some age-group football practices it's noticeable that the head coach has really not made clear the job of the people who are helping out. Have clear responsibilities for your assistant coaches. Designate position coaches and give them the responsibility for coaching their group. You'll find a great wave of enthusiasm from people who feel that they have a place of genuine contribution to the success of the team. Your team will be better served if all the coaches coach and don't feel like fifth wheels.

Discipline

During practice there will be times when players take a break or rest while you or your coaches are instructing. Players should use the "rest position," in which players kneel down on one knee. Players are resting but still are attentive to what the coaches are saying. Make all players aware that they should wear their helmets at all times—until you, or one of your assistants, tells them otherwise. Your players should never throw their helmets, sit on them, or leave them on the ground. Discipline problems, as they pertain to a player who is getting out of line with other players and coaches or who doesn't follow the rules, will result in the loss of playing time. If the problems continue, you might have to involve parents. Implement these rules at your first practice.

Practice Supplies Checklist

footballs: 10 to 12 needed to run an effective practice

whistles: one for each coach

scrimmage vests/helmet pinnies: you will need at least a dozen of either; when you are involved in group or scrimmage drills, these are used to distinguish offense from defense

kickoff tee/place-kicking blocks: you will definitely need one of each

blocking dummies: although you can run effective workouts without them, having at least four will greatly add to your teaching of basic blocking and tackling skills

first-aid kit: doesn't have to be a trainer's bag, but should have the basics, including ice or cold packs

water bottles: have each player bring one and have it labeled for private use

cones: a dozen or so 4- to 8-inch cones will do; these are used as boundaries for drills and as spacers for running backfield patterns

lined practice area: a full-size field is not always necessary to run a practice, but an area, lined to size, about 40 yards long should be available

practice plan: don't leave home without it

A Sample Practice Format

6:00 to 6:05

Line up: It's 6:00 P.M., and your team is ready to go. Position your assistant coaches, blow your whistle, and yell "Line up!" After you've taken attendance, you can begin your practice. Don't be discouraged if things go slowly the first practice or two. As soon as the routine becomes familiar, things will go much faster. If this is a second practice, or even a midseason practice, you might need to repeat the last exercise from your previous meeting. You may be pleasantly surprised how much the players remember!

6:05 to 6:12

Warm-up: You'll need to have your squad warm up their muscles before exercising. Some coaches send their kids on a lap or two, and that's fine. We suggest teaching even during the warm-up. One of the areas that's critical to all athletes is the ability to run efficiently. A player can be the biggest, toughest, strongest player on the field, but if he can't get to the spot to be big and tough and strong in time to use his skills, he won't be much help to his team. Use this period to warm up *and* teach form running.

Line up your team in groups of four on the boundary along a yard line and have players perform the following routine.

Striders (first time across the field). In this drill players try to get across the field in as few strides as possible. Have them count the number of strides it takes them and work to reduce that number each time they do the drill. This will help them to increase their stride length.

High knees, skips, and fast elbows (first time back across the field). Players divide the distance into thirds. For the first third they run so that their knees and thighs come up parallel to the ground. The number of strides is not important. As they cross the hash mark (inbounds marker) on the field, players switch to high-knee skips. Driving the knee up as high as possible, causing a high, exaggerated skip, is what we're looking for here. These two exercises also help with length of stride and help develop a more powerful leg action. The last third of the way back, players work on good arm action. Tell them to concentrate on bending their arms at a 90-degree angle so that their thumbs pass by their belts. Their hands should be perpendicular to the ground, thumbs up, and the arm action should be straight ahead and back, not side to side. Players should try to move their elbows as fast as they can. This helps increase their foot speed as the feet follow the arms.

Run on the line (second time across the field). As the players go back across the field, they concentrate on putting one foot directly in front of the other. This properly sets the foot on the ground for the most powerful pushing action. It also helps players run from point A to point B in a straight line without wobbling from side to side. Instruct players to keep their head still as they run. Simply put, all energy should be directed downfield toward the goal. Wobbling or bouncing wastes energy.

Form running (second time back across the field). On the last trip back players try to incorporate all the above drills into their running technique — putting it all together, so to speak.

6:12 to 6:25

Stretching: Exercise physiologists and trainers will tell you that you should never stretch a cold muscle. After form running, your team will be sufficiently warm for stretching. There are many different types of stretching routines, and most are good for the purposes of football. You may choose to have players partner stretch, which promotes teamwork and better concentration on the task of stretching but takes twice the time. However you stretch, make sure you hit all the major muscle groups, especially in the lower body. Remember to coach this period just as diligently as blocking or tackling. Walk through your lanes or around your circle of players and make sure they're doing the exercises in a proper manner and respect what they're doing. This is injury prevention time, and it's time well spent, but only if proper techniques are employed.

6:25 to 6:50

Fundamentals: Sometimes called *drill period*, this is the time when the basics are taught and reinforced. During this segment, individual skills are stressed. It's important to the progression of teaching that the skills you're demonstrating and drilling are related to larger group work and teamwork that are part of the rest of the practice. Teaching receiving drills to offensive linemen may be fun, but it won't get your linemen to where they need to be. Skills in this sport are position specific, and outside of recovering fumbles and tackling, most skills vary from spot to spot.

In this particular practice format, we've designated 25 minutes for teaching fundamentals. Don't take the whole time with one or two drills. Five to seven minutes for each drill is usually enough in a single dose. Move to something new, which will help keep your practice moving and create more sustained intensity.

6:50 to 7:05

Kicking game: This is the time for working on the various special teams involved in the third phase of the game. In preseason introductions, do only one type of kicking at a time, such as punting. Introduce the proper techniques to each player and have all players work on this portion of the game in a unit. As your players are placed on kicking teams and become more familiar with what is expected on these special teams, practice the offensive and defensive parts together: punt and punt return. This will ensure that you have your team prepared in all phases of the kicking game each week. If you're not going to use the place kick with your team, you can use this period once a week for special situations, such as offense for the end of the half or game, short-yardage plays, and goal line defense.

7:05 to 7:30

Group period: Offensive and defensive teams play as subteams as well as a total unit. Offensive linemen are sometimes referred to as the "team within a team," and backs need to work on coordinating their movements to enhance deception and confuse defenders. This is the time for these units to master their group assignments. Separate your groups so they won't be distracted by what's going on with the other group. If offense is your concern this practice, have your linemen work on the blocking schemes for the plays they'll practice when you bring the whole team together. You can have one set of players be the defenders for the other. You can also set up cones in the positions where you think that the opposition would be and have your players shadow-block them as a means of checking assignments. Make sure that you're speaking the language of football. Incorporate your starting signals when igniting your players into action and use a whistle to stop play.

The backs run the patterns of the same plays that the line is practicing. Small cones are useful to create proper spacing for the backfield alignments. Have a back drop to one knee to simulate the "snap" of the center to help with timing. Set up a goal line at least 10 yards from your drill and teach your backs to go full speed across the goal line. Teach them how to score.

You may want to mix groups. This teaches your backs to recognize their blockers and run through created openings. Centers and guards should work with fullbacks, while tackles and ends work with perimeter runners. Or, you may divide your line up into left side and right side with a set of backs. These all are common adjustments that can be easily done to enhance the learning process.

Your Other Job: Athletic Trainer

Injuries face every coach in every sport. It's a good idea to take a first-aid course; the American Red Cross has courses specifically designed for sport injuries. You should handle minor injuries as a good parent would. Move the drill or scrimmage away from the injured player, and move the player only when you're certain that moving will not cause further injury.

Contusions, bumps and bruises, sprains, and strains are facts of being in a contact sport, and although these are initially painful, most youngsters will be able to return to play in a short time. If the pain persists, use the RICE principle (see RICE sidebar, page 83) as the first line of action: rest, ice, compression, and elevation. Have your assistant coach attend to the affected player. Your coaching supplies should include at least two items: a supply of ice or cold packs and a 4-inch elastic bandage.

If your player is bleeding, separate him from the activity on the field. Your immediate concern should focus on three areas: bleeding, infection, and blood-borne pathogens. Again, be a good parent. Stock your first-aid kit with a variety of gauze and adhesive bandages, including butterflies and sterile pads, so you're prepared for injuries. Most bleeding caused from scrapes and cuts can easily be stopped with direct pressure with a clean dressing to the affected area. If this is successful, great! Be sure to clean the area and protect the wound with a gauze or adhesive bandage. If the bleeding does not stop, continue pressure and elevate the injury. Your player may require stitches to close the wound. Be sure to include latex gloves in your first-aid kit and to wear them when in contact with an open wound.

Unfortunately, some injuries can be serious and even life threatening. Although they're statistically rare, you and your assistants should be prepared for such injuries. Some, like broken bones, will be easy to recognize; others, such as concussions, are less obvious. Under no circumstances should you attempt to be an EMT (unless you are one already). Have a cell phone available and call for help. If the child's parents are not present, call them immediately. Separate the squad from the injured player and keep your players busy and away from him. Have your assistant stay with the injured youngster until his parents arrive. Include a cell phone and your phone call tree in your list of supplies.

When it comes to head and neck injuries, if the player says his head hurts or his neck feels funny, or worse, if he feels nothing, take no chances. *Don't remove the helmet!* Keep your hand on it to immobilize the area and call for help. Most of the time this is overkill, but you don't want to take any chances with any player's welfare.

Finally, document what you have done by keeping a record of any and all injury-related actions that you have taken. And no matter how minor an injury is, let the parents know about it. What seemed like a minor injury on the field can be very different later on.

If your workout has a defensive concentration, the same set of rules would apply, except there are three groups that need to be developed into a unit and then two groups coordinated together to mesh responsibilities in stopping offenses. Sometime after group work begins, defensive linemen work with the linebackers, and later, linebackers work with the defensive secondary.

Contact in this portion of practice needs to be controlled by the coach. Half-speed contact, called *thud*, is generally applied here, especially if you've had heavy-contact drills in fundamental time.

7:30 to 7:55

Team time: This is the scrimmage time of your practice. It's what the rest of your workout was pointing to. Players go 11 on 11, offense versus defense, and implement the plays on which the drills concentrated. Mastery of assignments is stressed, and corrections are frequent. Start from your huddle, tell your quarterback what you want, and let him call the plays. If it's defense you're working on, let your defensive signal caller make the calls and go from there.

7:55 to 8:00

Conditioning/cooldown: End your practice with an exercise in conditioning. Some coaches, especially early in the week, will have some extra work to keep the players in shape, such as 30-yard sprints. This is OK, but tone it down the closer it gets to game day. Have your players finish with some light stretching or a slow jog around the goal posts.

Leave them feeling positive: Try to finish on a positive note. Remember that your players are kids who love football and who are trying the best they can. It should make you feel good, too.

Sample Practice

Here's an example of what a practice might look like on paper.

Theme: Offense

Plays: Running game

Interior: Fullback Trap
Off Tackle: none today
Perimeter: Halfback Sweep

Formations

Pro
Slot
Double Wing

3:35 to 3:45 Form Running (whole team)

3:45 to 3:52 Stretching (whole team)

3:52 to 4:16 Fundamentals

Line: Coach Smith

3:52 to 4:00 Bird Dog **01**
4:00 to 4:08 Blocking Squares **02**
4:08 to 4:16 Pull and Trap **04** ; Pull and Lead **05**

Minor Injuries? Think RICE

For minor sprains and strains, the RICE method will help a minor soft tissue injury heal faster.

- **Relative Rest.** Avoid activities that exacerbate the injury, but continue to move the injured area gently. Early gentle movement promotes healing.
- **Ice.** Apply ice to the affected area for 20 minutes; then leave it off for at least an hour. Do not use ice if you have circulatory problems.
- **Compression.** Compression creates a pressure gradient that

reduces swelling and promotes healing. An elastic bandage provides a moderate amount of pressure that will help discourage swelling.

- **Elevation.** Elevation is especially effective when used in conjunction with compression. Elevation provides a pressure gradient: the higher the injured body part is raised, the more fluid is pulled away from the injury site via gravity. Elevate the injury as high above the heart as comfortable. Continue to elevate intermittently until swelling is gone.

QB/Receivers: Coach Jones
3:52 to 4:04 Quick Look **O9**
4:04 to 4:16 Focus **O10**

Backs: Coach Roy
3:52 to 4:00 Escape **O8**
4:00 to 4:08 Big Hitter **O6**
4:08 to 4:16 FB—Pull and Trap **O4** ; HB—Pull and Lead **O5**

4:16 to 4:31 Kicking Game Team and Punt Team

4:31 to 4:41 Water Break

4:41 to 5:01 Group Period

Line: Line scrimmage versus cones.
Backs and receivers: Run play patterns.

5:01 to 5:25 Team Time

Intersquad scrimmage: Run plays of the day and review old plays.

5:25 to 5:35 Conditioning

10-by-40-yard sprints by position.

Practice Overview

These time segments are subject to change as you make judgments on what skills and techniques your kids need and how long you want to devote to their mastery. But the elements of a practice—fundamentals, group work, special teams, and team scrimmage—should remain in each workout. Now that you have an idea of "when" to do things, we move on to the "what" and the "how" in the remaining chapters.

CHAPTER 8

Tips for Game Day

Game day is the time all athletes and coaches anxiously look forward to. Although your players are anticipating the fun of competition, you need to be concerned with the complete experience and to have your own thoughts and plans in order even before your players begin to arrive at the field. Preparation is the key here. We've listed in chronological order the tasks that need to be accomplished. We assume that field concerns at home and transportation needs for away games are taken care of by your noncoaching parents.

Depth Charts

We've already discussed the phases of the game as skills, positions, and alignments. In order to organize your squads, you need to have a depth chart for each team with your players listed in order of how they will be used: starter, first replacement, second replacement, and so on. Be sure to note if a particular player is a backup in more than one position or if a starter at one spot will have to move to another position if a replacement is needed. Charts should be made for each team and special team you plan to use. This is probably fairly straightforward for offensive and defensive teams for youth football, but remember that the kicking game is full of specialty teams. Make sure you complete charts for quick player replacement for all special teams as well.

Assign an assistant to make substitutions from these charts. Discuss how much leeway your assistants may use in substituting, so that you aren't surprised with "creative" teams on the field. It's good practice to have an assistant handle injury replacements as a part of his game duties. Remember that an injured offensive player may need replacements on a number of other charts as well. Organization is key: you don't want to waste a time-out in the game because only ten players go onto the field for your goal line defense, and you don't want to give up an easy touchdown because an injured player wasn't replaced on your punt team.

Game-Day Checklist

Tasks to Complete Before Game Day

Make depth charts for all personnel both offensively and defensively.

Make sure every player is placed.

Make depth charts for all kicking and other special teams. You should have at least two players placed at each position.

Establish a pregame itinerary for your staff and players. This should include:

1. Arrival time

2. Departure time if traveling

3. Start time for warm-up

4. End time for warm-up

5. Halftime location for team

Equipment and Supplies for Game

game ball, enough practice balls to run pregame, and kicking tees

depth charts for staff

first-aid kit

at least one of each type of player equipment, including belts and shoe strings and jersey

cooler full of ice

emergency communication (bring your cell phone)

small note pad (to jot down comments to players and to add to this list)

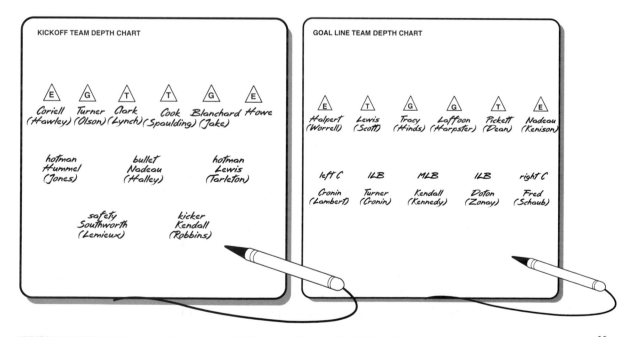

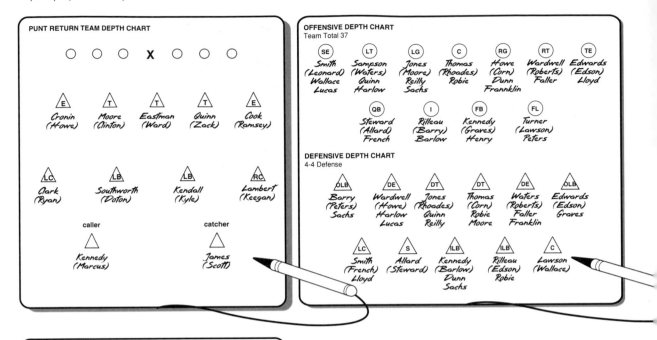

PUNT RETURN TEAM DEPTH CHART

○ ○ ○ X ○ ○ ○

E — Cronin (Howe)
T — Moore (Clinton)
T — Eastman (Ward)
T — Quinn (Zack)
E — Cook (Ramsey)

LC — Clark (Ryan)
LB — Southworth (Doton)
LB — Kendall (Kyle)
RC — Lambert (Keegan)

caller — Kennedy (Marcus)

catcher — James (Scott)

OFFENSIVE DEPTH CHART
Team Total 37

SE	LT	LG	C	RG	RT	TE
Smith (Leonard) Wallace Lucas	Sampson (Waters) Quinn Harlow	Jones (Moore) Reilly Sachs	Thomas (Rhoades) Robie	Howe (Corn) Dunn Frannklin	Wardwell (Roberts) Faller	Edwards (Edson) Lloyd

QB — Steward (Allard) French
I — Rilleau (Barry) Barlow
FB — Kennedy (Graves) Henry
FL — Turner (Lawson) Peters

DEFENSIVE DEPTH CHART
4-4 Defense

OLB	DE	DT	DT	DE	OLB
Barry (Peters) Sachs	Wardwell (Howe) Harlow Lucas	Jones (Rhoades) Quinn Reilly	Thomas (Corn) Robie Moore	Waters (Roberts) Faller Franklin	Edwards (Edson) Graves

LC — Smith (French) Lloyd
S — Allard (Steward)
ILB — Kennedy (Barlow) Dunn Sachs
ILB — Rilleau (Edson) Robie
C — Lawson (Wallace)

KICKOFF RETURN TEAM DEPTH CHART

G	T	C	T	G
Nadeau (Lynch)	Pickett (Halpert)	Lewis (Hummel)	D'Allah (Turner)	Laffoon (Scott)

E — Dunne (Eastman)
FB — Southworth (Heino)
E — Robinson (Hawley)

REC — Kennedy (Smith)
REC — Olson (Roy)

REC — Clark (Ferrigno)

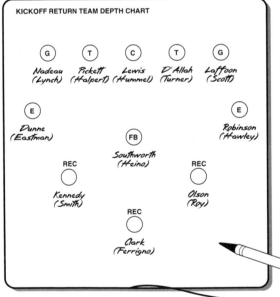

Some form of these charts should be ready as early as you can decide on players' positioning. Take a portion of the team time segment of your practice and rehearse this substitution procedure so no one is caught off guard when it occurs on game day.

Pregame Routine

The pregame warm-up period serves three functions: it warms up and stretches out the players' muscles and joints; it's a light practice that helps reacquaint players with the skills and assignments they need to perform in the game; and it establishes a mind-set that it's game time.

Begin the pregame practice as you begin a regular practice. Have a mild warm-up followed by a stretching period. Then have short, light drill periods in offense, defense, and kicking (you may want to have an earlier session with kickers, punters, long snappers, holders, and return players to warm them up before the general team warm-up). Quickly move to a group period and then a short team time. The whole routine should be about 30 to 45 minutes in length. Give your players time to get themselves mentally ready to play after the pregame is completed. Tell them what this time is for: personal readiness. How long this should be will vary with the age of your players. You'll be the best judge of the time needed. This is a very important period of time. Many times you'll be able to tell if your team is truly game-ready by watching them during this session.

Pregame Talk

No game was ever won by the pregame talk. If you've done a good job teaching and motivating your players at practices, and if you get a break or two, you have a good chance of winning. As far as your final talk to the team is concerned, try to keep your players on an even keel so they can expend their energy evenly over the course of the game: not too high when things go well and not too low when adversity appears. Remind them that the game is four quarters long and that they should concentrate on one play at a time. Be convincing and maybe a little forceful, but don't stay up at night watching Pat O'Brien or trying to come up with the right phrase for victory. What you don't want is your team to play in fear of making a mistake, which they will if they're afraid of the coaches' wrath. Be positive.

Bench Organization

Depending on the number of players on your team, it can be time-consuming to find the right player at the right time. If you have a rotation of players who go in and out of the game on a regular basis, have them follow you along the team area as you move with the ball. For the other players, have them sit or stand by position. This makes quick subbing easier. Assign an assistant as the bench coach. This isn't a full-time job, but it's nice to have someone watching over things. Give some of the players some bench responsibility as well. Being in charge of kicking tees and blocks, writing down plays, and keeping stats are fun things to do and can keep less skilled players interested and feeling important.

Game Planning and Play Selection

The process of game planning could take endless chapters in this book. Even at the high school level, hours upon hours of film study, staff meetings, and players' board work are required for coaches to be proficient in the proper preparation of a game plan. Translating the game plan into correct implementation on the field with all the adjustments and contingencies that occur is the science of coaching football. For our purposes here, it's wise to formulate what plays you're going to call in the game based on two factors: what your kids can do well and what kinds of weaknesses your opponent has. All of what we do is based on the same principle: the amount of time you want to expend on preparation is your limit on efficiency in this area.

Whatever you decide is right for you, think it out ahead of time. Write it down in an orderly fashion, work on it at practice, try most of it at least once in the contest, and refer to it continually during the game so you don't forget. We have provided five basic game day plays at the end of this chapter to get you started. Be creative with them. You can make any number of variations based on what you have learned from this book.

Most coaches send in plays with players. This is fine most of the time. Remember, you're limited in the time between plays, so it's a good idea to practice sending in plays. Additionally, if you need to, call a time-out. Generally speaking there are three time-outs per half of the game. These are good to use in a strategic situation, or just to gather your players to make sure everyone is certain of what they are supposed to do.

Substituting

If you plan to use everyone, then plan for it. You *can* give everyone playing time, no matter how little, by having a planned procedure for substitution. If you do this, you won't forget to play Chris or Pat. You can get them into the game early and maybe often if you plan things ahead of time. They'll feel important because they're not an afterthought. If you don't plan for them and include them, be prepared for the confrontation with their parents that will follow the game. The parents will be upset, and justifiably so; at the youth-league level, every child should play. Any number of players can be substituted between downs throughout a game. Just make sure the replaced players leave the field immediately and come back to your bench.

When you substitute because of poor performance, let the player know what he's done wrong and immediately tell him how to do it right. Be a teacher, not just a critic.

The question of changing quarterbacks is a common source of critical analysis by everyone except the starting quarterback's parents. Remember, by the nature of the position, you've given greater responsibility to this youngster because of his ability and leadership. You need to display your confidence in your decision by granting your quarterback greater latitude than other positions. When you think about it, every other player may be making the equivalent mistakes, but they aren't as visible as the child taking the snaps. However, you must strike a balance with team success. If you need to change quarterbacks you need to do so, but you also need to have someone on the field that the team will follow. On the offensive team, this leader needs to be the quarterback.

Halftime

Before the game begins, designate a place for halftime so that everyone knows where to meet. Make sure that your parent volunteers know where you'll be so that water and other halftime materials are waiting for you when you arrive.

No matter how good or how bad things are going, have a coaches' meeting first. Let the players rest. Then divide up your team by group for group meetings with each coach. Finish up with a talk from you to the whole team. During this talk you should be uplifting and positive in your approach to them and their efforts for the rest of the game. It's important to set a good tone for the beginning of the third quarter.

Postgame Comments

It's important to talk to your players immediately after the game. This should *not* be a time to critique their efforts. Be positive about their game and don't single out anyone. If they won, enjoy the victory. If they lost, pick out something positive about the team to leave them with. Remind them that getting up off the ground is a part of football and a part of life as well.

No matter what happens, win or lose, good practice or a bad one, finish positive. It's all about fun and being part of a team.

Developing Your Systems

You're going to have to develop systems for your team. These systems need to include the areas you want to attack, the basic methods you want to use in attacking them, and a way to communicate your wishes to the team. The systems of communication need to be as brief and concise as possible and at the same time simple enough to commit to memory.

Offensively, you may decide to use a complete number system and supplement it with word modifiers as needed. Some coaches number the gaps between linemen, starting from the center and numbering even to the right or odd to the left, and then numbering the backs 1 through 4. By simply calling "43," you can direct the 4-back to run through the 3-gap or "hole." Here's another example: by calling a "27-Counter," the 2-back (or slot back) runs counter (across the formation) and through the 7-hole.

Some use numbers to denote a series of backfield actions in the offense. The "20" series may describe a power game, and "26" is a power play through the 6-hole on the right side. Other coaches use words to describe the entire play: "Pro right tailback sweep right." No mistaking that intent. Numbers, however, have to be translated, while word calls can become long. There is no perfect system, but there are many workable ones.

However you choose to communicate your offensive thoughts, you'll need to have a menu of plays that present the defense with problems across the entire field. All effective offenses have the ability to attack each segment of the defense with well-thought-out and precisely coordinated maneuvers. In basic form, offensive football will need to have assaults on the defensive flanks, frontal attacks at the midsection of the defense, and slanting plays (between flanking attacks and frontal attacks). Along with these, a wise coach will have some countering moves that will take advantage of the opposition's tendency to react too quickly to initial offensive movements.

As a starting point in your thought processes toward developing a plan, let's look at two modes of thinking in attacking various spots on the defense, beginning with the flank. First, the simple approach: Draw a line between your center and guard on the side of the play. Number each offensive lineman on the play side of that line and then on the away side of the line. Now, looking at the defense, do the same, numbering them as they appear, both linemen and linebackers. Don't worry about the defensive backs at this point. What you will end up with is corresponding numbers on each side of the ball.

Now, tell each offensive lineman to block his corresponding number. Make sure players understand which direction the ball is going and tell them to block with the away-side shoulder if possible. If they can get this position on the defender they're blocking, they should swing their hips in the direction of the play, so that they're blocking away from the flow, and maintain contact until they hear the whistle. If they must block with the "wrong" shoulder, they should push hard toward the sideline and maintain contact until they hear the whistle. For the backs' role in this, put your best runner in the I-formation, where the backfield is lined up straight behind the center, behind your best blocking back. Don't be afraid to put this player deep to give him space to use his talents. Tell your blocking back to attack the flank and block the first defender to show. Tell him not to worry about which is the wrong shoulder. Tell him to match the intensity of the first defender and follow the golden rule: Maintain contact until he hears the whistle. Your quarterback turns and tosses the ball to the tailback and leads the sweep or fakes action in the opposite direction. It's very simple but effective if that tailback has the speed to make it go.

Need additional help at the point of attack? Have a guard with speed? Tell the guard that if his number is off the line of scrimmage, to pull to the play side and give some help. You have two guards with speed? Then tell the other guard to do the same thing. Now you have three blockers out in front of the ball carrier. Feel you are a little undermanned on the line or there is too much "flow" going to the point of attack, tipping off your intentions? Tell your blocking back (fullback) to fill for one of the guards. This can plug up some leaks in the line, plus give some misdirection to the play and maybe freeze some fast-flowing linebacker who now needs to stay at "home" to defend against a possible fullback blast up the middle.

Speaking of the frontal attacking game, let's look at this, again starting with the simple approach. The fullback blast up the middle is a great complement to the toss sweep. Your quarterback turns as he did in the toss play, but he now gives the ball to the fullback, who is filling for one of the guards, as mentioned in the previous paragraph. Your blocking can again begin with numbering the defense and understanding where the point of attack is. Remember, though, that your fullback has no lead blocker, so the sweep fake is critical to remove potential tacklers from the area. To help out this situation, you could try a trapping action using a switch in assignments between the two guards and the center. The center blocks the guard's man on the side to which the fullback is going. The away guard takes the center's block, and the other guard pulls and blocks that guard's man. Simply tell the center to follow his guard and look to create space. You can use the same principle you did in the toss play and lead the fullback ahead of the tailback up the middle.

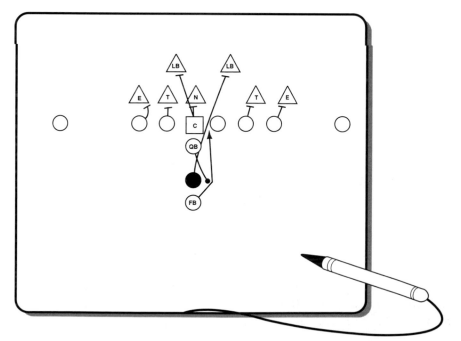

Linebacker isolation play. This off-tackle running play is designed to isolate your blocking back on the play-side linebacker.

The area between the sweeps and the middle is most often referred to as *off tackle*. Let's look at two simple ways of attacking in the off-tackle game. In the first scheme, we're going to isolate the play-side linebacker. We'll tell whichever lineman is his corresponding number to block on the nearest defensive lineman, either inside or outside, essentially double-teaming with the normally assigned player. The blocking back will lead block on the isolated linebacker. The rest of the line will recognize the point of attack and use the right shoulder/wrong shoulder principle on the respective assignments. This is the basic *isolation play* (see diagram previous page). You can also "blast" this area with the same principles used in the fullback blast scenario mentioned in the preceding paragraph. You could fill block with the fullback and pull either the play-side or away-side guard to add to the angle of the block or add some misdirection to your backfield action. If you want to be an "I" team (meaning your offense primarily lines up in the I-formation), these are probably just about all the running plays you need.

Game Day Plays

Here are five plays that will get you started on game day. You should make a point of coaching these in practice so that your offense becomes very familiar and comfortable with what their responsibilities are.

Basic sweep play. In this I-formation sweep, used against a 4-4-3 defensive (i.e., an eight-man front), the QB takes the snap and tosses the ball to the tailback. The tailback then runs toward the flank, trying to beat the defense to the outside. The offensive line attempts to reach block the appropriate defensive linemen in order to keep them from pursuing the tailback. The fullback is lead blocker, and the flanking back tries to reach block the call-side outside linebacker. Called in numbers, this play might be designated "Formation Right, 48"; in words it would be "Formation Right, Power Toss Right."

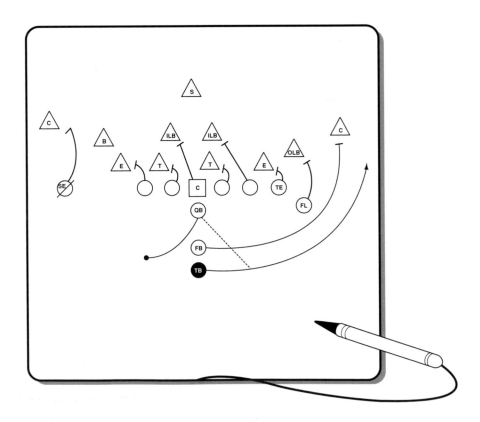

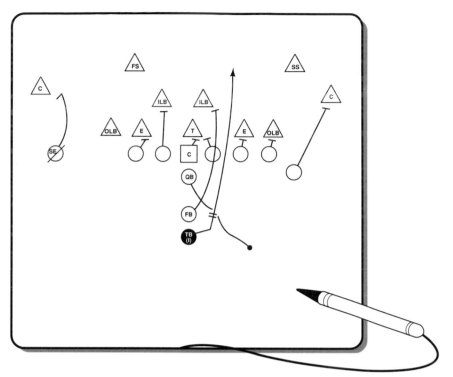

Basic isolation play against a 5-2-4 (seven-front) defense. In this I-formation play, the offense attempts to isolate an inside linebacker, leaving him unblocked while pushing adjacent defenders to the side. The fullback is now responsible for blocking the isolated ILB. The FB must maintain contact on the ILB so that the tailback can run through the created opening. In numbers: "Formation Right, 44." In words: "Formation Right, Iso Right."

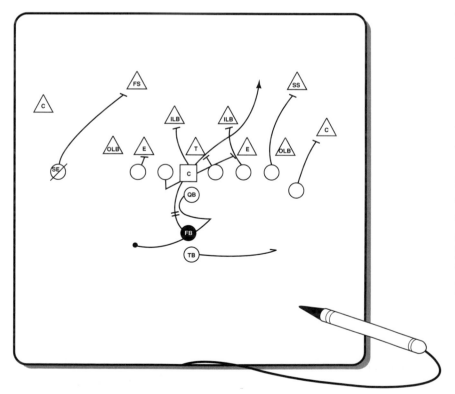

Basic trap play against a 5-2-4 (seven-front) defense. The three interior linemen use the pull-and-trap technique. The play-side tackle blocks the inside linebacker. The off-side tackle seals off the defensive end. The QB hands the ball to the fullback on the midline of the formation, while the tailback fakes the sweep play in the opposite direction. In numbers: "Formation Right, 32 Trap." In words: "Formation Right, Fullback Trap Right."

Basic counter play against a 4-4-3 or eight-front defense. The start of this play is very similar to that of the basic isolation play, but develops with the tailback countering to the backside of the formation. The off-side tackle pulls and traps, and his space is filled by the fullback. In numbers: "Formation Right, 43 Counter." In words: "Formation Right, Tailback Counter Left."

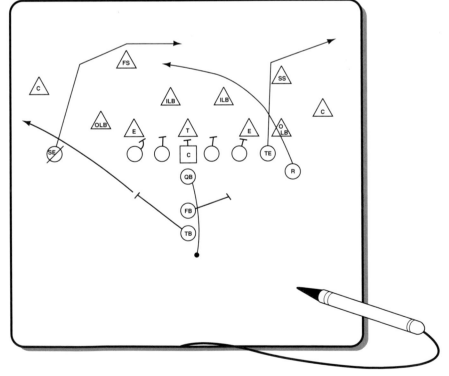

Basic drop-back pass, shown against a seven-front defense. The offensive line should pass block their area. The split end is the first route call, the tight end is the second route call, and the receiver is the third route call. The QB has a 5-step pass drop, the fullback will block the rushing outside linebacker (OLB), and the tailback will block the other OLB. If he covers a pass area, he will release from the OLB to become an outlet receiver. This is an advanced play. In numbers: "Formation Right, 524 Under." In words: "Formation Right, Pocket Pass Dig-Out-Under."

It should be pretty clear by now that the more effective the running game is, the easier the passing game becomes. The next progression would be to use running action plays as a disguise for throwing the ball. If we take the backfield action used in the off-tackle play, fake the ball to the tailback, have the quarterback retreat to pass, release an eligible receiver, and send a back out of the backfield, we have the beginnings of an effective play action pass. If we take our toss sweep play from earlier, have the quarterback attack the flank in the opposite direction, and send a receiver or two with him, we have an excellent "bootleg" pass.

If we want a drop-back passing attack, it's easily adaptable to any formation. Sound thinking for route development would be to have lots of crossing patterns, sharp routes, and deep passes for man-to-man cover teams and to teach receivers to find seams between defenders and short passes for zone cover defenses.

The K.I.S.S. Philosophy

Although neither of us could be accused of being great devotees of the K.I.S.S. line of thought ("keep it simple, stupid"), there's merit in keeping things as simple as possible in youth league. The balance to be struck, however, isn't always easy to find. Simple systems are simple to attack and defend, but mistake-prone football is problematic all by itself. In the end you have to be comfortable with yourself, your players' ability to learn, and the need to have a properly prepared team.

CHAPTER 9

Dealing with Parents

One of the most intriguing aspects of coaching is the reaction of parents to a game. After watching a poor team performance and a close loss, most parents react to the loss by saying, "Too bad they lost; they played a great game." After a great win, inevitably someone will come up with a less than enthusiastic congratulation. In the first example, the father saw his son play the game of his career, making tackle after tackle, hearing his name on the loudspeakers, and being recognized by the other parents who were near him in the stands. The second example demonstrates a mother who knows the team won a great victory, but she saw her son play only a small role that day and even watched him be chastised for a poor play. The difference for the coach is that he's looking at the big picture of squad performance and team success, whereas most parents, try as hard as they might, see little beyond their child. Even those parents who understand "role playing" in other endeavors, such as a school play, have a difficult time when it comes to athletics. This is normal and may be one of the reasons there wasn't a long list of volunteers for your position as coach. You should understand, accept, and be ready to deal with this reality. Unfortunately, you are at the level of athletics where this is the biggest problem. Although parental involvement and concerns become different as the level of participation goes up the scale, we all have a deep appreciation for parental influence.

No Room for Misunderstandings

On pages 7–8 we talked about creating a positive atmosphere for your team and letting the players know what is expected of them and what they can expect. In addition, you need to initiate early a positive atmosphere between you and the parents so that parents feel at ease discussing any issue with you involving the team and their child. This isn't always easily accomplished. Make sure all parents know your philosophy on practice time and attendance, on playing time and substitution policy, and on winning versus par-

Calling All Volunteers!

If you have parents who want to be part of the team but don't want to help out on the field, by all means use their enthusiasm to take over the administrative details. There are routine but important administrative aspects to running a team that could be taken over by a manager or several committed parents:

Phone Tree

Instead of having every kid call you whenever there's a threat of a shower or a change in the schedule, have one parent arrange a phone tree. You can call one designated person, who then initiates a reliable chain of communication for the rest of the team.

Practice Transportation

A designated parent can be in charge of carpooling by checking that each player has a ride to practice and home again. Though many families won't need this help, the safety net it provides for those who do is reassuring. This parent should make certain that all players are picked up from practice before he or she leaves.

Away-Game Transportation

It's a great idea to have a centrally located place where kids can meet before going to away games. A designated parent can schedule the time and place for meeting before away games and can make sure that there will be enough drivers to accommodate the players and that drivers have written directions to the field. Meeting like this before the game ensures that each player is accounted for and has a ride to the game, and it also builds team unity before the game.

Fund-Raisers

Getting all of the necessary equipment can be somewhat expensive. Having team dinners, organizing fund drives, and arranging other fund-raising events are projects that an administrative parent can organize, with some of the duties delegated to other team parents as well.

Snack Duties

A small, nutritious snack during practice or a trip to the ice cream stand after a game can be a helpful boost or well-deserved reward for your young players. A parent can be in charge of this service or can create a rotating schedule of parents who would be interested in helping. This is a fun and highly satisfying way that parents can become involved with the team.

ticipation. It's absolutely imperative that all parents in your program know what your coaching principles are, that you're always willing to talk to them about their child, and that you won't talk to anyone else about their child. Be ready to listen and calmly evaluate what they have to say, but stick to your principles. It may not be easy, but if you've given significant thought to what you truly want to accomplish and if you believe that these principles are in the best interest of your team as a whole, then these beliefs are worth standing up for.

It's important to let parents know how you feel about the forces that work on an athletic team, particularly when it comes to comments about coaches and teammates. Emphasize that whatever they have to say about everyone's play, you hope they'll help in your efforts to bring the players together, not pull them apart.

Declining Additional Help

Once you have found some volunteers and have planned your season, try to resist any additional help with the coaching, especially from those parents who only show up after your first game. These late additions tend to undermine those who have volunteered to put in the time to plan for the season, not only in their own eyes but also in the eyes of your players. Also, the youngster whose parent is new to the scene may be in the uncomfortable situation of teammate scrutiny, especially if his role on the team changes or he sees more playing time. Thank any new volunteers for their interest in coaching, and instead steer them toward volunteering for other duties.

Gender Issues

We don't think this will come as a surprise to anyone, but girls do play football—not in overwhelming numbers, but girls enjoy playing the game. Issues involving any condescending or sexist behavior should be dealt with as they occur.

We think that it's an injustice to their efforts to set up individual rules for girls in any activity and that individuals should be judged on how they contribute to the effort over any other consideration. Depending on the age and maturity of the girls involved, however, special protective equipment may be required for female players.

Questions and Answers

Q. Some parents come to practice and sit in their cars or just leave, but a couple of dads stand near their children and coach them during my practice. What should I do?

A. Telephone the parents directly and ask them to watch from off to the side or in the stands at practice time. Tell them that their sideline coaching may conflict with the techniques you're teaching and may cause their children friction with teammates. Make sure to phone these parents, rather than speaking to them on the field; a public request may be an embarrassment to the child.

Q. My neighbor's child wants to play football very badly, but his parents say they're concerned about his getting injured. How can I reassure them?

A. You cannot guarantee to anyone that any sport is injury free, especially a contact sport. You can say that all of the best equipment and safety precautions are being used. Add that the coaches are constantly observing players. If necessary, mention that despite all of the reports of injury, severe injury is rare and that playing with the team is infinitely safer than the drive to practice.

Q. I have a parent who constantly brings his son late to practice. I've spoken to him, but it's made no difference. This player is very good, but the other parents are resentful of his playing time. Should I punish the child by not playing him?

A. Unfortunately, yes. His playing is in direct opposition to your team rules and unity. His dad needs a wake-up call. Suggest to the father that his child could carpool to practice with other team members, thereby assuring the son will be there on time. Also, speak to the child directly to help him understand that rules are rules.

Q. A parent wants to talk about why her child is playing behind another child in a certain position. What can I tell her?

A. Discuss her child's positives and negatives, but under no circumstance should you discuss with her the other child, except to say you feel this child is deserving of his position.

PART TWO

Drills: The Foundation for Growth, Happiness, and a Coach's Peace of Mind

CHAPTER 10

Defensive Drills

This chapter provides the drills for the foundation of a solid defense. The skills and techniques learned will generate a defensive unit that works as a team. Introducing these one at a time, and working on them over consecutive practices, will help your players learn the different parts of team defense and understand how they work as a whole.

These drills are designed for players of all ages in youth football leagues. Be sure to include as many players as possible. There is a place for everyone and you'll need more than one player for each position.

Make sure to have fun!

Stance, Alignment, and Initial Drills

Alignment Check D1

Purpose: To teach the proper stance, alignment, initial, and take-off.
1. Have two stand-up dummies on either side of a coach with a ball (team-mates can be used for this, too). **2.** Just in front of each dummy, place three small 4-inch cones to represent the alignment techniques for each player. **3.** Have four lines of defenders on the other side of the ball. **4.** Call out the alignments for each session of the drill. **5.** Check alignments. **6.** Move the ball to simulate a snap and have the players strike the dummies. **7.** With the

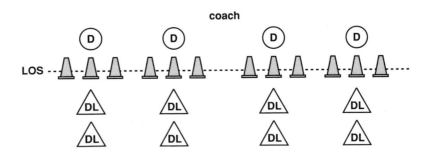

proper technique, players keep moving their feet until the coach blows the whistle to end the play. **8.** After each session change the alignment technique.

Coaching Points

1. Players keep their head up throughout the drill. **2.** They should strike the dummies quickly. **3.** Arms should be extended as contact is made (see chapter 4) to cause separation. (Separation is the term used to describe the act of moving away from a blocker. In this case, extending the arms should cause this separation.)

Stationary Mirror D2

Purpose: To teach proper stance.

Have linebackers face each other across the line of scrimmage and analyze each other as the coach goes up and down the line. The kids then critique each other, i.e., "Keep your head up and your hands forward," etc. They mirror each other so they can see what they're doing right and wrong.

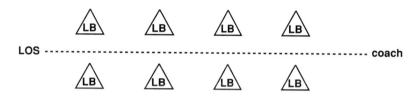

Coaching Points

1. Make sure all players' heads are up. **2.** Look to make sure their backs are straight. **3.** Check the shoulder-width stance. **4.** Hands should be above their waists and out in front. **5.** Their eyes should be on their opponent (their mirror).

Quick Step D3

Purpose: To teach linebacker initial.

1. Set up four lines of linebackers and have the first player in each line be an offensive lineman. Have the defenders at linebacker depth. **2.** Position a coach on the offensive side of the drill with two lines on each side of him. **3.** The coach simulates a snap and moves the ball to one side or the other to indicate direction of a running play or raises the ball in passing action to indicate a pass. **4.** Offensive players move straight out toward the linebacker, and the linebacker steps up to meet them, executing initial, creating space or separation, and shedding the blocker. **5.** After each session, the linebackers move up in line and switch from defense to offense.

Coaching Points

1. The coach should snap the ball first and then quickly move in the intended direction. **2.** Linebackers position their heads on the direction

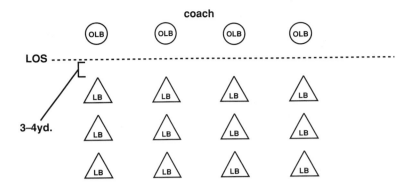

side. **3.** Start out the drill with all players doing the same thing so that each player can master the techniques. Go from run, side to side, then to pass. **4.** Proper techniques are the important lessons here.

Pursuit D4

Purpose: To teach the relentless pursuit of a ball carrier.

1. Arrange your team into defensive units. **2.** Use a "young" coach as the ball carrier/passer. **3.** Position coaches near the sideline about 15 yards downfield with a ball. **4.** Set up cones to simulate an offense and place a ball next to the center. **5.** Have the first group in a huddle and the other unit in a huddle off to the side. **6.** Call a defensive set, break the huddle, and go to alignment and stance to defend the cone offense. **7.** The ball carrier/passer simulates a snap, runs around one flank or the other of the cones and up the sideline, or drops back to pass. **8.** If it's a run, the players react with initial technique through their gap of responsibility and pursue the ball carrier until *everyone* on the team touches the player-coach (hence the need for a "young" coach). **9.** If it's a pass play, the passer either throws or simulates throwing in the direction of one of the coaches. The receiving coach either catches the ball or has a ball to toss and catch (to simulate a reception). Again, every player then sprints toward the ball, and *everyone* gets a hand on the receiver.

Coaching Points

1. Tell your players never to follow one of their teammates, but to take their own path directly to the ball carrier. **2.** Don't use a whistle to end the play, since the drill ends when the last person touches the ball carrier.

Tackling Drills

Our advice is to work backward. Start with the moment of contact and then increase the distance and intensity once the question of "what am I going to do when I get there" is understood.

Fit Position Tackling D5

Purpose: To teach proper tackling technique.

1. Pair up your players by size; one is the tackler, and the other is the player being tackled. **2.** Put the tackler in the "Fit" position—that is, with the shoulder in the waist area of the runner, the arms squeezing him, and the hands holding the jersey in the back. **3.** On the whistle, the carrier tries to break free, while the tackler tries to bring him to the ground.

From this drill a progression can develop. Again moving backward, start the drill one step away. Then try it three steps away and allow the carrier to have a ball. Next create a tunnel with cones and give the carrier some latitude to change direction. After this, change to a wider tunnel and extend the distance to 5 yards. Because the rest of tackling is getting to the point of controlled movement, there's no need to make the distance any greater. However, you need to explain the concept of control, breakdown step, and gathering. These are the transitions from full-speed running to the point 5 yards from the carrier. From the sprint, the defender begins (control) to widen and shorten the strides (breakdown) and lower the center of gravity (gather).

Coaching Points

1. Players keep their eyes up and wide open. **2.** They square up their hips to the goal line. **3.** They take short, choppy steps. **4.** Players make their tackles by "climbing" the runner and grabbing his jersey.

Interception Drills

Transition (Zone or Man-to-Man) D6

Purpose: To teach defensive backs to move from initial to coverage.

1. Line up your defensive backs several yards behind a yard line, which will serve as a line of scrimmage. Have a coach face the line of backs from the quarterback's position. **2.** Have the first defensive back in line take alignment off the coach if in zone transition, or add a route runner if in man-to-man transition. **3.** In zone transition, the coach simulates a snap, and the player goes into initial; as the coach raises the ball in passing action, the defensive back makes a crossover run to the side of the intended pass, always watching the ball. **4.** In man-to-man transition, a route runner will be added as a reference for the defensive back, rather than the coach's movement. **5.** Coach both zone and man.

Coaching Point

1. Players should get depth quickly. **2.** Players should follow the ball or focus on the route runner.

Reaction Time D7

Purpose: To teach defensive backs to react to the release of the ball.

1. Line up the defensive backs behind the 25-yard line. A coach stands on the 10-yard line. **2.** As the coach raises the ball to throw, the first defensive back in line goes into a crossover run watching for and following the intended pass direction. **3.** The coach throws the ball, and the defensive back reacts to the location, moves to the point of intersection, intercepts the ball, yells "Bingo!," and returns to the closest hash mark and stops. Repeat the process with each defensive back.

Coaching Points
1. Remind the back to catch the ball at its highest point possible; in other words, meet the ball. **2.** Make sure to emphasize to your defensive backs that during games, they should run to the nearest hash mark and, if possible, score. **3.** Remind the defensive (intercepting) team to treat the interception like a punt return as soon as they hear "Bingo."

CHAPTER 11

Offensive Drills

This chapter provides the basic drills that break down the concepts of offensive football. These drills are designed for players of all ages in youth football leagues. Take the time to teach them: there is a lot to learn. Teaching the skills individually will enhance the performance and understanding of the offense as a whole.

Be sure to include as many players as possible. There is a place for everyone and you'll need more than one player for each position. Make sure to have fun!

Stance and Takeoff Drills

On pages 62–63, we discussed the importance of the proper stance. The stance is only important for affecting this critical phase of line play. Whatever stance you choose, it needs to be a launching platform for controlled aggression. It needs to be mastered. Drills will help your linemen win this critical first challenge to the success of your team.

Bird Dog 01

Purpose: To teach proper stance, cadence, and initia steps.
1. Arrange your linemen (OL) into four lines, with each line 3 feet apart and with 6 feet between players.
2. Use a cadence call to begin the drill (the same call the QB would start the offense with. Example: "Hut-one, Hut-two, Hut-three" or "ready, set, go!"). **3.** Walk around and check the stance of your players. **4.** Have your linemen work on a quick first step in every direction on your signal and then quickly get back into their stances. **5.** Now repeat, adding a second step, and have your players quickly reset. **6.** Finish up with the first step in the technique for pass blocking.

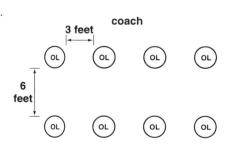

Coaching Points
1. To help teach players to stay low, have them press their chest to their thighs on the first step. **2.** Check to make sure there are no false steps during this drill.

Blocking Squares 02
Purpose: To teach blocking techniques.
1. With cones, create a 6-foot square on the field and mark the spot where the diagonals intersect. Make more than one of these blocking squares if you have more cones, that way you can involve more players. **2.** Put a defender (DL) or a dummy inside the perimeter of the square and an offensive lineman (OL) outside the square. **3.** On a snap count have the blocker execute the block you're drilling and have him block the defender out of the square. Players start at position 1, and the blocker moves the defender left to right. Players move to position 2, and the blocker drive blocks the defender backward. Then players move to position 3, and the blocker moves the defender right to left.

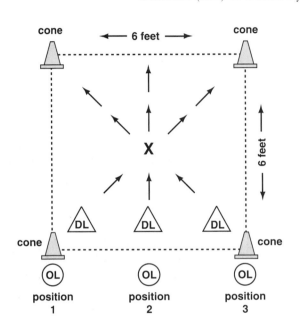

Coaching Points
1. Start off with dummies held by players and give passive resistance so that the player finishes the skill. **2.** Gradually add resistance. **3.** Pair up players by size for full resistance. **4.** Players maintain contact and leg drive until the defender is out of the square.

Onion 03
Purpose: To teach pass blocking.
1. Before using this drill, diagram it as shown opposite to show your players how the drill works. **2.** On the field, draw a large "onion-top" cross section, measuring 7 yards from the LOS to the top, and place a dummy (your pretend QB) at the top. **3.** Draw four lines from the LOS to the top of the onion 5 yards apart. **4.** Place four offensive linemen (OL) inside the onion and four defensive linemen (DL) outside. **5.** On command, defenders attempt to "sack" the dummy, while the blockers work to keep the passer untouched.

Coaching Points
1. This drill promotes quickness out of stance to the blocking position.
2. The offensive linemen keep the inside position and ride the defenders

out. **3.** Encourage the linemen to keep their arms locked out and their backs straight. **4.** The blockers must stay in the lanes of the onion. **5.** Players maintain contact until the whistle blows.

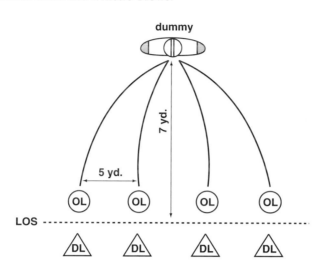

Good sequence of pass blocking drill versus bag. The players are on their knees in order to isolate their arm techniques.

Pulling and Trapping Drills

Pull and Trap O4

Purpose: To teach linemen trapping techniques.

1. Establish a line of scrimmage and set up four dummies or defenders on the defensive side. Place three offensive linemen (OL) on the other side of the line of scrimmage. **2.** Align the blockers on the first three dummies.

3. On command, the blockers block as assigned, with the first blocker pulling and trapping the first free dummy. **4.** Use block angle (top diagram) and drive block (bottom diagram) techniques for nonpulling linemen. Rotate blockers.

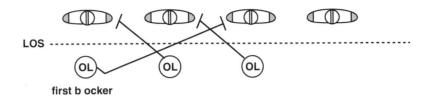

first b ocker

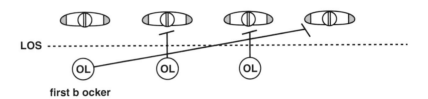

first b ocker

Coaching Points
1. The pulling lineman blocks with his outside shoulder, keeping his head toward the line of scrimmage. The technique is to pull right and hit right. **2.** Vary angle and drive techniques to help the puller recognize a free defender. **3.** Switch the pulling drill from right side to left side after every blocker has gone through the drill. **4.** Players maintain contact until the whistle blows.

Pull and Lead 05
Purpose: To teach linemen perimeter pulling techniques.
1. Establish a line of scrimmage and place linemen on either side of the ball. **2.** Place a 4-inch cone at the tackle spot at a deeper depth than the linemen and lay dummies down at the flank to form a lane going upfield. **3.** Place a dummy or defender at the top of the lane and one at the end of the lane. **4.** On command, the two offensive linemen (OL) pull toward the lane. The first blocks the first free defender or dummy, and the second takes the remaining defender or dummy.

Coaching Points
1. Blockers should pull with depth to avoid possible congestion at the LOS (which is typical in a game situation). **2.** Blockers should keep their head upfield. **3.** Switch the drill from side to side. **4.** For a variation on this drill, if the first dummy is removed by the coach, the first pulling lineman turns

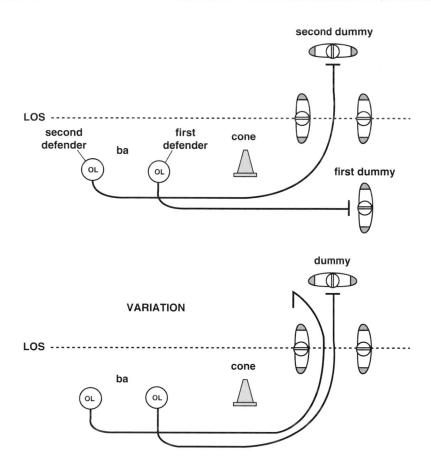

up in the lane and attacks the next defender, while the second pulling line-man follows and then looks inside and then outside for other possible defenders. This should be done as the drill is in progress to teach pulling recognition skills and downfield blocking. **5.** Players maintain contact until the whistle blows.

Running Drills

Big Hitter 06
Purpose: To teach backs to deliver hits with the free arm and maintain balance.
1. Line up three or four defenders, dummies, or players with shields (a handheld dummy that looks like a shield), 5 yards apart and 3 yards from the sideline. **2.** Five yards away have a line of ball carriers (BC) facing them with footballs. **3.** One at a time, the carriers attack the defenders, running between them and the sideline and delivering a blow with their free arm. **4.** After all players have had a turn, the ball carriers turn around and repeat the drill using the other arm. **5.** Relieve the defenders with replacements.

OFFENSIVE DRILLS

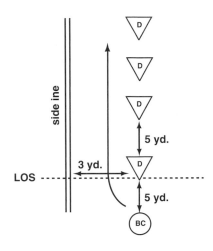

A good example of the Big Hitter drill.

Coaching Points

1. The ball carriers look for a good *gathering point*—the point at which they coil to deliver a hit to the defender. **2.** Carriers should stay low. **3.** As the carriers get better, gradually increase the resistance from the defenders.

A good example of the Stiff Arm drill.

Stiff Arm **07**

Purpose: To teach backs how to ward off defenders.
1. Pair up defenders and ball carriers across a yard line.
2. In each pair, the defender gets into position to tackle, and the ball carrier puts his hands on the defender's helmet. **3.** Use a cadence call to start the drill. **4.** The defender attempts to tackle the ball carrier, who pushes the defender's head down and away from him and tries to avoid contact.

Coaching Points

1. Ball carriers keep their arms stiff throughout the move. **2.** They bring their inside leg through before pushing the defender's helmet down. **3.** Ball carriers continue running 5 yards to complete the move.

Escape **08**

Purpose: To teach runners to avoid contact.
1. Create a blocking square (see **02**). **2.** Place a defender with his heels on the back line opposite the ball carriers. **3.** The ball carrier (BC) is 2 yards outside the box. **4.** The carrier runs into the box, and the defender attempts to tackle him before he escapes from the box. **5.** The carrier can go out any side of the box except the side from which he entered. **6.** Both players can move on the signal to begin.

Coaching Points
1. Have the runner concentrate on the defender's belt buckle and feet.
2. The runner should make his final move when the defender's weight comes up or he puts his weight on one foot.

Receiving Drills

Quick Look 09
Purpose: To teach catching skills and quick reaction.
1. Pair up your receivers 5 yards apart, and give each pair a ball. **2.** With the players facing each other, they throw the ball to their partner. **3.** When it is caught, they immediately tuck in the ball, turn, and make a move as if to run for the end zone. **4.** A variation is for one player to turn his back to the other, who has the ball and is the passer. The passer says "right" or "left" and releases a soft pass. **5.** The receiver turns to the called side and catches and tucks the football.

Coaching Point
1. Check for proper thumb position before and after the catch.

Focus 010
Purpose: To teach focus and concentration on the catch.
1. Line up your receivers just outside the end line and the goal post. Have your passer(s) out around the 5-yard line facing toward the back of the end zone. **2.** One at a time, receivers run along the end line, from one sideline to the other, so that the goal post is between the passer and the catchers. **3.** The passer times his throw so that the ball passes the goal post as the receiver is running behind it. **4.** The receiver concentrates on the ball even as the post interrupts his vision. **5.** After running his route, the receiver returns the ball to the passer and then goes back and gets in line to run the drill again.

Coaching Points
1. A dummy can be used instead of a goal post. **2.** If your passer continually hits the goal post or dummy, tell him to aim at it. He'll be more likely to miss it then.

Handoff Drills

Hand Off and Hit 011
Purpose: To teach handoff technique and proper vision.
1. Make a line of your backs behind each of your quarterbacks. **2.** Have one back hold a shield near the line of scrimmage (or use a dummy). **3.** The coach stands between the lines of players in order to observe. **4.** On a

cadence call, practice the exchange between the quarterbacks and the ball carriers. The ball carrier then delivers a blow to the shield-holding back (or dummy) and spins away from contact.

Coaching Points

1. The ball carrier should focus on the bag and not the handoff. **2.** The quarterback should reach for the back and shouldn't swing the ball up to him.

Quarterback–running back alignment during the Hand Off and Hit drill.

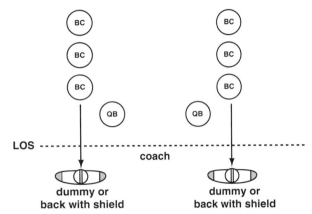

Mixed Group Drills

Sometimes it's important that skills from different groups be brought together to blend techniques. Here are some common mixed-group arrangements you might want to use in your practice time.

Centers and Quarterbacks 012

Purpose: To work on the exchange (the "snap") between the center and the QB.
1. The quarterback holds the ball with his throwing hand across the laces and stands behind the center, who is in his stance. **2.** The center reaches back through his legs, takes the ball from the quarterback with both hands, and carefully brings it to the position where it will rest in on the line of scrimmage. **3.** The quarterback, with his thumbs together, places his throwing hand under the center's rear end, palm down and with pressure up, creating a seal. His elbows and knees are bent, ready to follow the center forward as he steps to execute his block. **4.** The center executes the exchange, on the cue from the cadence, by reversing the previous handoff sequence as fast as possible. **5.** The quarterback brings the ball into his stomach, with his elbows tucked in tightly, and begins the play action.

OFFENSIVE DRILLS

Coaching Points
1. The center makes sure that as he delivers the ball, the laces come into contact with the quarterback's fingers. **2.** The QB brings the ball in tight to his stomach with his elbows tucked in close to his sides.

Skeleton 013
Purpose: To eliminate extraneous players in order to concentrate on specific assignments.

Coaching Points
Despite their name, skeleton drills are not specific drills. Rather, the term applies to any drill where all nonessential players are removed from the drill so that only key players participate. These drills help players see just how important their assignments are to the success of any particular play and they show them the importance of their role as a member of the team.

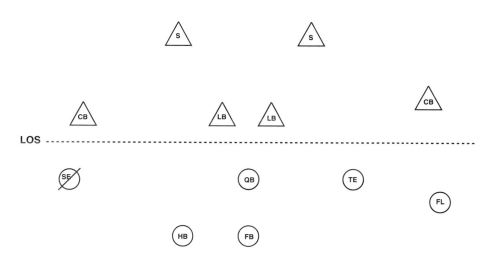

Example of a skeleton "drill." Here all defensive linemen and all interior offensive linemen are eliminated so that the offensive backs and receivers and the defensive backs can concentrate on their respective assignments without distraction.

Half Line 014
Purpose: To teach timing.
1. Divide up the offensive line into right side and left side, with a set of eligibles with each (see diagrams next page). **2.** Switch sides and groups so that the backs can get the timing down with the line in half the time.

Coaching Points
The drawback to half-line drills is that they tend to give the message that the away side of a play is not important, sometimes leading to poor downfield blocking. If you use this form of drill, use some time for back-side blocking downfield.

Half-line drills. Run the right and left sides of the offensive line in alternating 5-minute intervals, practicing sweeps and off-tackle runs.

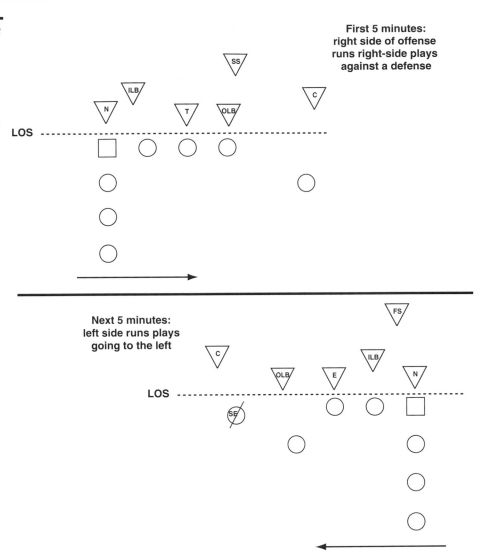

First 5 minutes: right side of offense runs right-side plays against a defense

Next 5 minutes: left side runs plays going to the left

Passing Drills

One-Knee Passing   O15

Purpose: To teach proper hip rotation and ball position.
1. Put your quarterbacks opposite each other about 7 to 10 yards apart.
2. The quarterbacks put their throwing-side knee down and extend their lead foot forward. **3.** Using correct ball position and an exaggerated motion, the players throw the ball to their partner.

Coaching Point
1. Check for good rotation and follow-through.

Fast Drop 016

Purpose: To help the quarterback develop a timely pass drop and quick delivery.
1. Place three quarterbacks on a line about 5 yards apart. **2.** Position three receivers 10 yards in front of the quarterbacks and number them receiver 1, receiver 2, and receiver 3. **3.** Have one quarterback call cadence to begin each session, such as "Hut-one, Hut-two, Hut-three . . . " **4.** The quarterbacks retreat whatever number of steps you've established and set up for passing. **5.** Call out the number 1, 2, or 3 of the hot receiver. **6.** The quarterback affiliated with the receiver of that number then throws to that receiver. The second quarterback throws to one of the remaining receivers, and the third quarterback must find the last open receiver.

Coaching Points
1. Quarterbacks should practice proper foot movement and gather technique. **2.** They need to react to receivers quickly. **3.** Rotate the order in which the quarterbacks pass the ball. **4.** When the basic drill is mastered, start adding pass patterns to the drill.

CHAPTER 12

Kicking Drills

As you've learned by now, kicking is a very important part of football and the overall strategy of the game. The success of your kicking program will be largely dependent on the age and skill level of your players. Keep in mind that your players are never too young to start learning. These basic drills will help teach how to defend the kick your offense has just made and how to kick the ball properly. These drills should be a steady part of your practice diet.

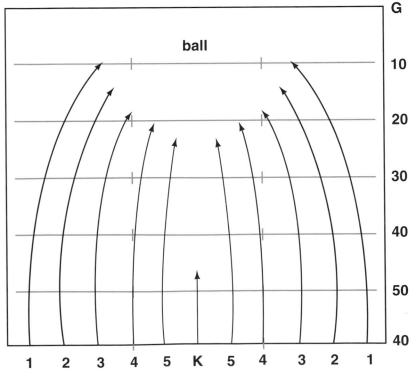

ball

Lane Coverage K1

Purpose: To teach lane responsibility on the kickoff.
1. The kickoff team lines up to kick and the receiving team sets up to receive.
2. On the coach's whistle, the ball is kicked and the players run downfield in their lane of responsibility.
3. The lanes should adjust to the direction of the ball.

Coaching Points
1. "Stay in your lanes" is the most important coaching point to emphasize to your players. **2.** If the ball is kicked to one side, the lanes adjust to become small on the kick side and wider on the away side. **3.** Outside

players are responsible for making the running area narrower by forcing the runners to their inside. **4.** Discipline is an absolute must in single-line coverage, as one leak can let the receiver get by, spelling disaster. To forestall a leak, one player, maybe the kicker, should stay back as a safety.

Perfect Contact K2

Purpose: To walk a punter through the mechanics of punting.
1. Two punters stand 15 yards apart and face each other. **2.** Using perfect form (see How to Find and Select a Punter sidebar on page 73), the two play catch by punting to each other.

Coaching Points

1. The kicking foot should be flat, with the toe pointed, and the ankle flexed. **2.** Watch for good follow-through. **3.** Work on punts that spiral; they shouldn't tumble end over end. Practice and repetition are the keys here!

APPENDIX: Referee Signals

Illustration courtesy National Federation of State High School Associations

Ball ready for play *Untimed down	Start clock	Time-out Discretionary/injury time-out (follow by tapping hands on chest)	TV/Radio time-out	Grasping face mask or helmet opening
Touchdown Field goal Point(s) after touchdown	Safety	Ball dead Touchback (move side to side)	First down	Helping runner
Loss of down	Incomplete forward pass Penalty declined, No play, No score, Toss option delayed	Legal touching of forward pass or scrimmage kick	Inadvertent whistle (Face Press Box)	Interlocked blocking, Illegal use of hands or arms (NFHS), Illegal block in the back (NCAA)
Disregard flag	End of period	Sideline warning	First touching (NFHS) Illegal touching	Player disqualification
Uncatchable forward pass (NCAA)	Encroachment (NFHS) Offside defense (NCAA)	Illegal procedure (NFHS) False start, Illegal formation Encroachment offense (NCAA)	Illegal shift—2 hands Illegal motion—1 hand	Tripping

Delay of game	Substitution infraction	Failure to wear required equipment	Illegal helmet contact	Clipping
Unsportsmanlike conduct Noncontact foul	Illegal participation	Sideline interference	Running into (NCAA) or Roughing kicker or holder	Blocking below waist Illegal block
Illegal batting/kicking (Followed by pointing toward toe for kicking)	Invalid fair catch signal (NFHS) Illegal fair catch signal	Forward pass interference Kick catching interference	Roughing passer	Chop block
Illegal pass/forward handing	Intentional grounding	Ineligible downfield on pass	Personal foul	Holding/obstructing Illegal use of hands/arms (NCAA)

Glossary

Alignment: By placing imaginary numbers on the shoulders and heads of the players on the offensive line, the defense will know what stance to take. Alignment is part of the first step of a good defense.

Angle block: A technique used by the offensive line that starts with a short directional step and then contact. Once momentum is achieved, the blocker can maneuver the defensive player in the intended direction.

Audible: A play called by the quarterback at the line of scrimmage that changes the play previously called in the *huddle*. Also a change of plans in game play just before the ball goes into play.

Balanced line: An offensive formation with an equal number of linemen on either side of the center.

Blitz: An all-out run by linebackers and defensive backs, charging through the offensive line in an effort to *sack* the quarterback before he can *hand off* or pass the ball.

Block: An offensive maneuver in which the blocker uses legal contact to prevent the defender from getting to the ball carrier.

Bootleg: The quarterback fakes a handoff to backs going one way while he goes the other way to run or pass.

Boundary: Also known as the "sideline" or "out-of-bounds."

Bullets (hot men): Lead defenders on the kickoff team. They are not restricted to lanes and their primary focus is converging on the ball carrier.

Cadence call: This is the keyword in the *offensive play call*, used by the quarterback in the *huddle*, to let the center know when to snap the ball. Here's a sample offensive play call: "Pro, Rip, 26 Cross, on One." After the quarterback informs his offense of the play in the huddle, when he comes to the line the call might sound like this: "Down, Set, Hut!" On "Hut!", the ball is snapped. Had the QB said, "Pro,

Rip, 26 Cross, on Two," he would have called, "Down, Set, Hut, Hut!" And so on.

Center: Responsible for snapping the ball to the quarterback, which signals the start of a play.

Chain gang: Three assistants to the officials whose job is to handle the first-down measuring chain and the *down box*.

Check off: Calling an *audible*.

Clipping: Blocking or hitting an opponent, other than the ball carrier, from behind, typically at leg level. Clipping is a foul and results in a 15-yard penalty.

Clothesline: Striking another player across the face with an extended arm. This is a personal foul and results in a 15-yard penalty.

Completion: A legally caught pass.

Conversion: See *point after touchdown*.

Corners/cornerback: Modern corners are primarily defensive backs who defend against the pass. A later arrival on running plays, corners defend the ball in the air.

Curl/curl in: A maneuver where the receiver runs downfield before turning back to run toward the line of scrimmage.

Dead ball: A ball that is no longer in play; that is, a ball that is not held by a player or loose from a kick, fumble, or pass.

Defense: The team defending against the *offense*.

Defensive backfield: The area or players behind the defensive linemen. The defensive backfield is the last line of defense against the offense. Consists of two safeties, two cornerbacks, and three or four linebackers.

Delay of game: Failure to begin a new down within 25 seconds of the ball being put into play. This is a foul and will result in the loss of 5 yards.

Depth chart: A listing of players by position by their skill and ability.

Down: An offensive play, starting with a center snap and ending when the ball is dead. The offense gets four downs to gain 10 yards. Each time the team gains 10 yards, it earns a first down and has another four downs in which to gain another 10 yards.

Down box (down indicator): A seven-foot metal rod, on the end of which are four cards (numbered 1 to 4), used to keep track of the number of the down being played.

Down and distance: A simple reference to what the current down is and how many yards are needed to get the first down. Example: "third and 10" means it's the third down and 10 yards are needed to get a first down.

Down and in: A maneuver where the receiver runs straight downfield and then suddenly cuts toward the middle of the field.

Down and out: The opposite of a *down and in*. In a down and out, the receiver runs downfield and then turns out, toward the sideline.

Draw play: A fake pass that ends with one of the backs carrying the ball after the defensive linemen are "drawn" in on the pass rush.

Drive block: Used by the offensive line to push defenders straight back and away from the line of scrimmage.

Eligible: An offensive player who is legally able to catch a forward pass; that is, the player is "eligible" to receive the pass.

Encroach: Defensive player entering the *neutral zone* prior to the snap. This is a foul and results in a 5-yard penalty.

End line: The ends of the field, where the goal posts are located.

End zone: The area between the *goal lines* and the *end lines*; the last 10 yards at either end of the field.

Extra points: After scoring a touchdown, a team can earn one more point by making a successful *place kick*, or it can earn two more points by running a successful scrimmage play from the 3-yard line into the *end zone*.

Fair catch: On a *punt* or *kickoff*, a receiver is protected from being tackled by indicating he will catch the ball and not advance after catch-ing it. The player signals a fair catch by raising his hand and waving it from side to side just before the catch.

False start: The offense, prior to the beginning of the down, makes movement toward the line of scrimmage that resembles the start of a play. This is a dead-ball foul and results in a 5-yard penalty on the offense.

Field goal: A *place kick* taken during a scrimmage down that goes over the crossbar and between the upright bars of the goal posts. A field goal earns the offensive team three points.

Field position: The ball's location on the field.

Flanker: An offensive player on the right or left side of the formation. A flanker usually plays as a receiver and is split out wider than a wing back.

Flood: An attempt to swamp the opposition or an area of the field with sheer numbers of receivers.

Formation: The arrangement of the offensive players at the beginning of each play. There are many formations, including the "punt formation," "I-formation," "T-formation," and "wishbone formation." These are generally named for the shape of the formation. For instance, an I-formation involves two running backs in an I-shaped line behind the quarterback; the wishbone formation has the two halfbacks on each side of the fullback set back a few yards; and the T-formation has all three backs in a line parallel to the line of scrimmage.

Form running: Incorporates all running techniques that are learned from running drills. These include striders, high knees, skips, fast elbows, and running the line.

Forward pass: A pass thrown "forward," or in the direction of advancement (toward the opponent's goal).

Foul: A breaking of the rules. Common fouls are *holding* (grasping an opponent who doesn't have the ball), personal fouls (tripping an opponent or striking an opponent with one's hand, knee, or head), *interference* (a defensive player stopping the completion of a pass or kick by contacting the receiver before he has the ball), *clipping* (pushing an opponent in the back), and face mask (grabbing an opponent's face mask).

Four-down territory: The designated area of the field when using all four downs to either gain the first down or to score is strategically sound. See also *three-down territory.*

Four-point stance: A lineman will put both hands on the ground, creating a four-point stance. The feet are staggered about heel to toe and spread slightly wider than the shoulders. It and the *three-point stance* are typical for linemen.

Free kick: The kick taken to start or restart play. Used after a team has scored and includes the *kickoff* and the kick after a safety.

Full House alignment: See *Straight T alignment.*

Fumble: A ball that is dropped while in play.

Gap: The space between adjacent offensive linemen.

Goal line: The line at each end of the field 10 yards from the *end lines* over which the ball must pass to score a touchdown.

Goal-line stand: Making a stand against the opposition at or near one's *goal line* in a tough defensive effort.

Gridiron: Another name for a football field.

Hail Mary: The quarterback throwing the ball up in the air without really targeting any particular receiver and hoping someone on his team catches it. This pass is typically thrown at the end of a half or game.

Hand off: To hand the ball off to a teammate.

Hash marks: Marks that divide the field into thirds width-wise. Whenever the ball becomes dead on or outside one of these marks, it is placed on its respective hash mark.

Holder: The player who holds the ball during a *place kick.*

Holding: Illegally keeping another player from advancing by literally holding him back with one's hands. This is punishable by a 10-yard

penalty if the holding call is against the offense, and a 5-yard penalty plus a first down if it's against the defense.

Hook: A pass route in which the receiver heads straight downfield, and then abruptly turns back toward the line of scrimmage.

Hot men: See *bullets.*

Huddle: The grouping of the players to plan the next play. As a noun, the group itself.

I-formation: See under *formation.*

Illegal motion: Forward movement by an offensive player before the snap, or having more than one man in motion at the snap. This is a foul and results in a 5-yard penalty.

Inbounds marker: The spot where the ball is placed after a play has been completed. Also known as a *hash mark.*

Incomplete pass: A *forward pass* that is not caught or intercepted.

Initial: The first reaction to the movement of the offense, especially for defensive linemen, is critical to winning. Initial is the second step of a good defense.

Intentional grounding: The quarterback purposefully throwing the ball out-of-bounds or into the ground to avoid throwing a bad pass, which might be intercepted or to avoid being *sacked* by the defense. Intentional grounding can be difficult to call, but a referee may assign the offending team a 5-yard penalty and the loss of their down.

Interception: When a defender catches a ball thrown by the opponent's quarterback in the air. Results in a *turnover*, with the defense becoming the offense.

Interference: Offensive interference occurs when blockers run in front of a running back. Defensive interference (or defensive pass interference) occurs when a pass defender interferes with a receiver trying to catch the ball and usually when the defender is unable to intercept the pass. For example, interference is called when a defender has his back to the ball, sees the receiver he's covering is readying to catch the ball, and then waves his arms in front of the receiver to distract him.

Jamming: The act of bumping or corralling a receiver by the defensive secondary in an effort to disrupt a receiving pattern or route.

Key: Watching a player to attempt to see the direction in which the player is going to move. A player may make small movements such as foot placement that can give away his next move to an observant player who is keying him.

Kick: Attempting to score a *field goal* or *point after touchdown* by kicking the ball.

Kickoff: The kicking team (determined by a coin toss) kicks the ball from the free-kick line (the 35-yard line in pro football, the 40-yard line in high school and college). This is the start of the game.

Lateral: A pass that is thrown in any direction other than toward the opponent's goal.

Line judge: An official who keeps track of time and also watches for various violations, including the quarterback's position when passing (the quarterback isn't allowed to go past the line of scrimmage to pass).

Line of scrimmage (LOS): An imaginary line, running from sideline to sideline through the front point of the ball, on which players line up at before the start of play on each down.

Live ball: A ball that is still in play. A live ball is either loose as a result of a kick, fumble, or pass or it's held by a player.

Man in motion: A player who turns and runs behind the line of scrimmage and parallel to it as the signals are called. He then runs downfield just as the ball is snapped.

Man-to-man defense: Covering each member of the offense with a member of the defense. Also called "player-to-player defense." See also *zone defense*.

Multiple offense: Offensive strategy using a number of formations.

Neutral zone: The space between the line of scrimmage and a parallel line that runs through the rear point of the ball.

Nickel defense: A defensive formation involving five defensive backs.

Noseman: Also known as a "nose tackle." Generally the player who defends the *center*.

Numbering system: The system used to number players' uniforms according to their position. Although only offensive players are required to be numbered by position, numbers are assigned as follows: 1 to 19, quarterbacks and kickers; 20 to 49, running backs and defensive backs; 50 to 59, centers and linebackers; 60 to 79, defensive linemen and offensive linemen; 80 to 89, wide receivers and tight ends.

Offense: The team with the ball; the offense attempts to run or pass the ball across the defense's *goal line*.

Offensive backfield: The area or players behind the offensive linemen. These are the running backs, the quarterback, and a second wide receiver.

Offensive play call: A typical play call is made up of five parts: the formation, the motion, the back and hole number to be attacked, the type of play or series, and the *cadence call*. For example, a play called in a *huddle* might be this: Pro (formation), Rip (motion), 26 (back and hole number), Cross (type of play or series type), on One (the cadence call).

Offside: Crossing the line of scrimmage on the opposing team's side before the ball is snapped. This is a foul and results in a 5-yard penalty.

Off tackle: The area between the sweep area and the middle of the formation is called the off tackle. This is typically the area of focus for the isolation play.

Onside kick: A short kick of at least 10 yards that the offensive team hopes to recover and gain some yardage with.

Open up holes: To push the opposition aside by blocking them in an attempt to create space in their defense through which a runner can pass with the ball.

Option play: An offensive play where the player

with the ball has the option of running or passing.

Outside: Toward the sideline.

Overtime: An extension of playing time to break a tie. In pro ball, the first team to score into overtime wins. This is known as the "sudden death" system.

Passing game: The offensive strategy dealing with throwing the ball and receiving *forward passes*.

Passing tree: *Passing patterns* and running routes for receivers.

Pass pattern: The specific route run by a receiver to catch a pass.

Pass rush: The rush by the defense to tackle the quarterback before the ball is thrown.

Penalty: Punishment for a foul resulting in losing a down or even the ball. A penalty usually sets back the penalized team 5 to 15 yards.

Perimeter play: A play run to the outside, or perimeter, of the line of scrimmage.

Pigskin: Old term for a football.

Piling on: Several players jumping on the player with the ball after he's been tackled. Also called "dogpiling." Piling on is a foul and results in a 15-yard penalty.

Place kick: A kick made while the ball is held in place on the ground (either with a tee or by another player).

Play: In general, the actions of the players following a snap or kickoff. More specifically, the type of action taken as part of a planned maneuver. There are two basic types of plays: "running plays," where the offense tries to run with the ball toward the opposition's goal line, and "passing plays," where the offense tries to pass the ball forward toward the opposing goal line. A play can have minor variations each time but will usually fit into some general categories. For instance, in a *sweep*, the guards pull from their positions to block for the ball carrier as he moves left or right and then up the field. In a *draw play*, the quarterback takes the ball from the center and moves back

rapidly, acting as though he's going to throw it. When the defensive linemen get close, the quarterback then hands off the ball to a running back who tries to quickly dart past the defensive linemen, who are still being "drawn off" by the quarterback. In an "action pass," the opposite occurs; the quarterback pretends to hand off the ball to another player but retains the ball and attempts to complete a pass.

Play action: A passing play set up to draw the defensive linebackers toward the line of scrimmage with a running fake before the pass.

Playbook: A notebook containing a team's terms, strategies, plays, and so on, issued to each player.

Pocket: The area in which the quarterback sets up his pass. This area is guarded against the opposition in an attempt to form a safe "pocket."

Point after touchdown (PAT): After scoring a touchdown, a team may score an extra point for a successful *place kick* through the opposition's goal posts. Also called a "try."

Post pattern: A *pass pattern* where the receiver runs 10 to 15 yards downfield before turning toward the middle of the field, at a 45-degree angle in the direction of the goal posts.

Power I: For a strong inside running game, one of the stronger running halfbacks is often brought back and placed behind the fullback. This creates an extremely strong side for an offensive attack.

Primary: The receiver chosen to receive the pass.

Pro formation: A classic pro formation entails using one of the offensive backfield positions as a receiving player by flanking him like a split end.

Pulling: Leaving one's position to move elsewhere to block.

Pump fake: The quarterback drawing back his arm and faking a forward pass to draw the free safety to an area or to cause a defensive back to pause in his coverage of a wide receiver.

Punt: Kicking the ball by dropping it and kicking before it hits the ground.

Punt return: To run back the ball after a punt.

Pursuit: After recognizing what the offense is trying to do and understanding the responsibilities they have, the defense should take the most direct route to the ball. This is the fourth step of a good defense.

Quarterback sneak: A play where the quarterback receives the ball after the snap and immediately runs forward through the opposition, with his own team blocking for him.

Quick count: The quarterback calling the signals at the line of scrimmage very rapidly so as to throw off the other team.

Quick kick: A surprise punt.

Ready list: A list of several plays ready to be used in an upcoming game (tailored to an opposing team's strengths and weaknesses).

Recognize and react: The defense's ability to recognize what the offense is going to do on any one play and where they need to be to stop it. This is the third step of a good defense.

Recover: Grabbing a ball that has been fumbled (whether the recovering player's side initially had the ball or not).

Red zone: Strategically, this designated area of the football field extends from the defense's goal line out to the 20-yard line and is considered to have the highest scoring probability for an offense. All four downs should be used for scoring attempts either by *touchdowns* or *field goal* attempts.

Returner: A player who runs back *kickoffs* and *punts*.

Reverse: An offensive play in which the player with the ball runs in one direction and then hands off the ball to another player going the opposite direction, thus reversing the ball's direction of travel.

Roll: A movement to the left or right by the quarterback before throwing the ball.

Roster: A list of the members of a team.

Roughing: Illegally contacting another player, as in "roughing the punter," when a player tackles the punter without touching the ball, or "roughing the passer," when a defensive player attempts to tackle the quarterback after the ball has been thrown. This is a personal foul and results in a 15-yard penalty.

Run back: Returning a *kickoff, punt,* or *interception.*

Rush: To run from the line of scrimmage with the ball.

Sack: Tackling the quarterback before the ball is thrown.

Safety: Forcing the opposition to down the ball in their own end zone, resulting in two points for the defense. Also, the player position called "safety" is a defensive backfield position, the deepest in the backfield. There are two safeties.

Safety blitz: A charge by one or both safeties in an attempt to tackle the quarterback.

Safety valve: A short pass thrown to a running back when the wide receivers are covered.

Scramble: When a quarterback runs behind the line of scrimmage and attempts to lose tacklers.

Scrambler: A quarterback who has gotten a reputation for scrambling.

Screen pass: A pass from behind the line of scrimmage, after a deep drop by the quarterback. It's a play that allows the rushers to charge through as the offensive linemen fake-block them, only to set up a wall for a receiver or running back to catch the pass and run behind.

Scrimmage: The action between two teams, starting when the ball is snapped.

Secondary: The defensive backfield, or second line of defense.

Shift: The movement of two or more offensive players between positions.

Signals: A system of words or numbers called by the quarterback to tell the other players what the next play will be. Signals are also used at the line of scrimmage to tell the center when to snap the ball.

Slant: Running straight out and then at an angle prior to catching the ball. A pass pattern.

Slot: A gap in the offensive line between a receiver and a tackle.

Snap: The handing of the ball by the center, as he reaches back between his legs to the quarterback or punter.

Special teams: A special group, or "platoon," of players specializing in one particular maneuver, such as *punts* or *kickoffs*. When the maneuver is about to be done, the coach substitutes the special team. Also called "bomb squads" or "suicide squads" because of their higher injury rates.

Split end: A receiver who lines up several yards away from the next player along the line of scrimmage.

Spread punt: A standard punt formation with 15 yards between the long snapper and the kicker.

Sprint-out passing game: This is a passing style where the quarterback, after receiving the snap, runs to the flank instead of dropping straight back. This gives him the choice of either running or throwing.

Square in/out: A pass route where the runner goes downfield and then *turns in* at a "square," or right angle to the center of the field, or *turns out* to the sideline.

Squib (pooch) kick: A low, flat *kickoff* that is difficult to handle. It is often used when the receiving team has an effective kick returner or when the kicking team does not have a long-ball kicker.

Stance: How a player lines up in position: one hand down on the ground, two hands down, or no hands down. Different positions require different stances. For example, a defensive lineman would likely be in a *three-point stance* (one hand down), while a defensive back would likely have no hands down and be in a balanced *two-point stance*. Stance is also the second half to the first step of a good defense.

Straight (stiff) arm: To defend against a player trying to tackle you by using your hand and arm to jab with a straight stiff arm at the opponent's head or chest area to avoid a tackle.

Straight T alignment: An offensive alignment where all three backs are in a straight line, behind the quarterback, and parallel to the line of scrimmage. Also known as a "Full House."

Strong side: In an unbalanced line, the side with the most players.

Stunt: An unusual charge by the defensive linemen, sometimes in concert with the linebackers, in which they loop around each other during the charge instead of charging straight ahead.

Substitution: Putting a player into the game as a substitute for another. For example, a play requiring a very fast player may cause the coach to remove one player and replace him with another, faster player. There is quite a bit of substituting in football, especially with special teams.

Succeeding spot: Used when assessing penalties. As opposed to the previous spot, where the play started, the succeeding spot is where the play ended. Some penalties bring the ball back to the line of scrimmage (where the play started) and some bring the ball to the succeeding spot (where the play ended).

Sweep: See under *play*.

Tackle (intercept): The fifth step of a good defense. The defense should follow the ball and either make a tackle on the ball carrier or try to intercept a pass.

Tailback: A member of the offensive backfield, whose job is to run with the ball. Also called a running back or halfback.

T-formation: See under *formation*.

Three and out: The term used to describe an offense that, while in possession of the ball, was unsuccessful in gaining 10 yards and a first down. That is, the offense used three downs to try and gain the first down, and used the fourth down to punt the ball away.

Three-down territory: A strategically designated part of the football field where an offense would use three downs to try and gain the first down, and it would use the fourth down to punt the ball away. If the offense used the fourth down to try and get a first down and was unsuccessful, the ball would be turned over to the opposing team, which would then have very good *field position* in terms of a scoring opportunity. Using all four downs in the three-down territory is considered very risky and would most likely be used only if a team was trailing and it was the fourth quarter with very little time left on the play clock.

Three-point stance: The position of players at the line of scrimmage before the snap, in which they lean forward on one hand with their feet spread.

Thud: A half-speed contact technique used in practice. It's not full-contact, nor is it a *tackle*.

Tight end: A receiver positioned next to a tackle on the end of the line formation.

Tight punt formation: Used when kicking from your own goal line, meaning the space between players is reduced and there is not the standard 15 yards between the long snapper and the kicker.

Touchback: The defensive team gains possession of the ball in their own end zone on the same play in which the offensive team caused the ball to cross the goal line.

Touchdown: Carrying the ball into, or catching the ball in, the opposition's end zone. It scores six points.

Trap block: When a player is allowed through the enemy line only to be blocked by surprise from another player behind the line. Also called a "mousetrap."

Turn in/out: A pass route where the player runs downfield and then turns in toward the middle of the field or out toward the sidelines.

Turnover: Losing possession of the ball, typically by error.

Two-point stance: A balanced stance with weight only slightly over the toes, every joint slightly flexed, and the hands resting on the tops of the thigh pads.

Unbalanced line: A formation with more players on one side of the center than the other.

Under zones: The area of the field between the line of scrimmage and the deep zones.

Wall return: A formation, generally a wedge shape, used by the kick return team to create a blocking "wall" for the return player.

Weak side: The side of an unbalanced line with the least players.

Wide-out: A term sometimes used for the fastest deep-threat wide receiver on a team and sometimes for the wide receiver who's furthest from the ball when it's being snapped. See also *flanker* or *split end*.

Wing formation: A variation to the Straight T and the Power I that entails moving a halfback to a flanking position on the tight-end or split-end side. To secure both flanks, backs can be placed in the wing position on both sides of the formation.

Yardage: The amount of yards gained or lost during a play.

Yards after catch: Term used to describe the yards gained by a receiver after the ball has been caught.

Zone defense: A defense strategy where each player has an area, or "zone," of the field to defend. See also *man-to-man defense*.

Resources

Associations and Organizations

American Football Coaches Association (AFCA)
100 Legends Lane
Waco TX 76706
254-754-9900
E-mail: info@afca.com
www.afca.com
Formed, in part, to "maintain the highest possible standards in football and the profession of coaching football," and to "provide a forum for the discussion and study of all matters pertaining to football and coaching," the AFCA stands as the single entity solely representing all levels of football and the football coaching profession.

American Sport Education Program (ASEP)
1607 N. Market St.
Champaign IL 61820
800-747-5698
Fax: 217-351-2674
E-mail: asep@hkusa.com
www.asep.com
Offers educational courses and resources for coaches, directors, and parents to make sports safer, more enjoyable, and valuable for children and young adults.

National Alliance for Youth Sports (NAYS)
2050 Vista Pkwy.
West Palm Beach FL 33411
800-729-2057; 800-688-KIDS
(800-688-5437); 561-684-1141
Fax: 561-684-2546
E-mail: nays@nays.org
www.nays.org
This organization sponsors nine national programs that educate volunteer coaches, parents, youth sport program administrators, and officials about their roles and responsibilities. It's Web site provides information on these education programs, including: PAYS (Parents Association for Youth Sports); NYSCA (National Youth Sports Coaches Association); NYSOA (National Youth Sports Officials Association); START SMART; and the Academy for Youth Sports Administrators.

National Athletic Trainers' Association (NATA)
2952 Stemmons Fwy., Suite 200
Dallas TX 75247-6916
800-TRY-NATA (800-879 6282); 214-637-6282
Fax: 214-637-2206
www.nata.org
NATA's mission is to enhance the quality of health care for athletes and those engaged in physical activity, and to advance the profession of athletic training through education and research in the prevention, evaluation, management, and rehabilitation of injuries.

National Federation of State High School Associations (NFHS)
P.O. Box 690
Indianapolis IN 46206
800-776-3462 (to order rule books); 317-972-6900
Fax: 317-822-5700
www.nfhs.org
Publishes rule books for high school sports, case books (which supplement rule books), and officials' manuals.

National Football Foundation (NFF)
22 Maple Ave.
Morristown NJ 07960
800-486-1865; 973-829-1933
Fax: 973-829-1737
E-mail: membership@ footballfoundation.com
www.footballfoundation.com
A multifaceted not-for-profit educational organization dedicated to the promotion of amateur football, its character building attributes, and the fostering of these qualities in the development of scholarship and leadership. Through a network of 118 chapters located throughout the nation and a membership of over 10,000 strong, the NFF supports a number of initiatives, which promote the game, preserve its history, and ensure its future. The chapters emphasize the educational benefits associated with football and provide educational opportunities for parents, players, and coaches.

National Strength and Conditioning Association (NSCA)
1955 N. Union Blvd.
Colorado Springs CO 80909
800-815-6826; 719-632-6722
Fax: 719-632-6367
E-mail: nsca@nsca-lift.org
www.nsca-lift.org
Seeks to unify members and facilitate a professional exchange of ideas in strength development as it relates to the improvement of athletic performance and fitness. The NSCA provides its members with a wide variety of resources and opportunities designed to enhance their education and careers, including: professional journals, conferences, scholarship and grant opportunities, educational texts and videos, and career services.

National Youth Sports Safety Foundation (NYSSF)
1 Beacon St., Suite 3333
Boston MA 02108
617-277-1171
Fax: 617-722-9999
E-mail: NYSSF@aol.com
www.nyssf.org
A nonprofit educational organization whose goal is to reduce the risks of sports injury to young people.

North American Youth Sport Institute (NAYSI)
4985 Oak Garden Dr.
Kernersville NC 27284-9520
800-767-4916; 336-784-4926
Fax: 336-784-5546
www.naysi.com
NAYSI's Web site features information and resources to help teachers, coaches, and other youth leaders, including parents, interact more effectively with children around sports. It includes a resource section that lists books on sports and coaching, as well as two interactive sections where browsers can submit questions on fitness, recreation, and sports. The Web site's newsletter, Sport Scene, focuses on youth programs.

Positive Coaching Alliance (PCA)
c/o Stanford Athletic Dept.
Stanford CA 94305-6150
650-725-0024
Fax: 650-725-7242
E-mail: pca@positivecoach.org
www.positivecoach.org
PCA is transforming youth sports so sports can transform youth.

Women's Sports Foundation
Eisenhower Park, East
Meadow NY 11554
800-227-3988
Fax: 516-542-4716
E-mail: wosport@aol.com
www.WomenSportsFoundation. org
A charitable educational organization dedicated to increasing the participation of girls and women in sports and fitness and creating an educated public that supports gender equity in sports.

Web Sites

American Youth Football (AYF)
www.americanyouth football.com
An international youth football organization established to promote the wholesome development of youth through their association with adult leaders in the sport of American football. Rules and regulations are established to ensure that players play in an atmosphere of safety with a competitive balance between teams.

C.O.A.C.H.
www.coachhelp.com
Comprehensive online access to coaching help.

Coach Illustrated
E-mail: comments@Coach Paterno.com
www.CoachIllustrated.com
Football coaches at every level can educate themselves by attending online clinics 24 hours a day—covering everything from skill improvement drills, offensive and defensive schemes, building a successful program, and game preparation to dealing with today's players.

Coaching Clinic
www.eteamz.com/tobys/ coclinic.htm
Online football coaching clinic allows you to send your question, comment, or answer

for posting. It's a great way for coaches to exchange ideas with a large number of people.

Coaching Youth Sports

www.tandl.vt.edu/rstratto/CYS
Virginia Tech's Health and Physical Education program sponsors this Web site, which provides coaches, athletes, and parents with general, rather than sport-specific, information about skills for youth. The site also allows browsers to submit questions.

Footballcamps.com

E-mail:info@footballcamps.
  com
www.footballcamps.com
Web site run by Sports International that provides football camp listings for children from 8 to 18.

Infosports.net

http://infosports.net/football
The football section of the InfoSports Web site features tournament listings, teams looking for tournaments, football message boards, and a database of football knowledge compiled from the contributions made by the visitors to this Web site.

National Women's Football League (NWFL)

E-mail: dreamfootball@cs.com
www.nwflcentral.com
Founded in August 2000 to provide the opportunity for women to play full-contact football in a well organized and professionally run league.

National Youth Sports Coaches Association (NYSCA)

800-729-2057; 800-688-KIDS
  (800-688-5437); 561-684-
  1141
www.nays.org/coaches/index.
  cfm
NYSCA trains volunteer coaches in all aspects of working with children and athletics. In addition to training, coaches receive continuing education and insurance coverage and subscribe to a coaching code of ethics.

National Youth Sports Officials Association (NYSOA)

800-729-2057; 800-688-KIDS
  (800-688-5437); 561-684-
  1141
www.nays.org/officials/nysoa.
  cfm
Trains volunteer youth sports officials, providing them with information on the skills required, fundamentals of coaching, as well as common problems they may encounter.

NFLHS.com

E-mail: nflhs@nfl.com
www.nflhs.com
The NFL Web site for youth and high school football. Offers news on professional players, tips and drills, fitness, academics, and NFL programs. Links also to the NFL

Youth Football Fund, which is a nonprofit foundation run by the NFL/NFLPA that seeks to use football as a catalyst to promote positive youth development and also ensure the health of grassroots football in future generations.

Officiating.com

E-mail:
Feedback@Officiating.
  com
www.officiating.com
Offers news, updates on rule changes, coaching philosophy and mechanics, and discussion boards.

Parents Association for Youth Sports (PAYS)

800-729-2057; 800-688-KIDS
  (800-688-5437); 561-684-
  1141
www.nays.org/pays/index.cfm
Provides material and information for youth sports programs to help teach parents about their roles and responsibilities in children's sports activities.

PE Central

E-mail: pec@pecentral.org
http://pe.central.vt.edu
This Web site is designed for physical education teachers, parents, and other youth workers. It provides the most current information on appropriate physical education programs, helping young people on their way to a lifetime of physical fitness and health.

USAfootball.com
www.usafootball.com
Provides coverage of youth, high school, National Collegiate Athletic Association (NCAA), National Association of Intercollegiate Athletics (NAIA), National Junior College Athletic Association (NJCAA), semi-pro, and professional football. It strives to cover traditional American football at all levels, producing a positive impact on scholastic and collegiate competitions and is dedicated to increasing the media exposure of women's football.

WeTeachSports Inc.
www.weteachsports.com
WeTeachSports.com offers the best educational materials available anywhere on all kinds of sports.

The Zone—A Football Coaching Site
www.coachingfootballonline.
  com
A noncommercial Web site intended to provide football coaches of all levels a resource to communicate with other coaches around the world.

Football Stores and Publications

American Football Monthly Magazine
P.O. Box 13079
North Palm Beach FL 33408
800-537-4271; 800-556-2632
Fax: 561-627-5275

www.americanfootballmonthly.
  com
The only trade journal for the football coaching professional.

American Football Specialists
P.O. Box 50484
Bowling Green KY 42102
270-843-8393
E-mail:RickSang@Prokicker.
  com
www.propunter.com;
  www.prokicker.com
Football products for punters and kickers.

Coaches Choice
P.O. Box 1828
Monterey CA 93942
888-229-5745
Fax: 831-372-6075
E-mail:info@coacheschoice.
  com
www.coacheschoice.com
One of the world's largest publishers of books and videos for coaches.

The Coaching Store
197 Woodland Parkway #104-
  526
San Marcos CA 92069
877-553-2214; 760-734-4819
Fax: 760-727-0824
www.thecoachingstore.com
A store for youth sports coaches.

Football America
12061 Tech Rd.
Silver Spring MD 20904
877-MY-SPORT (877-697-
  7678); 301-625-7700

Fax: 800-322-1763
E-mail: info@footballamerica.
  com
www.footballamerica.com
Football equipment store, retail and online.

Goal Sporting Goods
P.O. Box 236
Essex CT 06426
800-334-GOAL (800-334-
  4625)
Fax: 860-767-9121
www.goalsports.com
A supplier of goals and field equipment.

Gridiron Strategies
P.O. Box 624
Brookfield WI 53008-0624
800-645-8455; 262-782-4480
Fax: 262-782-1252
E-mail: info@lesspub.com
www.lesspub.com/gridiron
A resource for football coaches at every level of competition written by football coaches for football coaches. Published six times a year, each issue offers the latest strategies, plays, ideas, and management tips to help you build a successful program.

Index

Numbers in **bold** refer to pages with illustrations. The glossary and resources have not been indexed.

About the Authors

Paul Pasqualoni earned a B.S. in health and physical education from Penn State, and a M.S. in physical education and human performance from Southern Connecticut State College. He has run one of the nation's leading football programs for twelve years. In that time, Syracuse has had six victories in eight bowl game apperances. He lives in DeWitt, New York, with his wife, Jill, and their sons, Dante and Tito.

Jim McLaughlin played football and baseball for Southern Connecticut State College. He has coached at the high school and collegiate level for over thirty years. As a high school football coach for the last thirteen years, his teams have been to the state finals eight times, winning three state championships.